FOR ORGANS, PIANOS & ELECTRONIC KEYBOARDS

**197**

# Acoustic Classics
## 34 Songs of the '60s and '70s

ISBN 0-7935-8238-5

HAL•LEONARD
CORPORATION

7777 W. BLUEMOUND RD. P.O. BOX 13819 MILWAUKEE, WI 53213

Visit Hal Leonard Online at
**www.halleonard.com**

## CONTENTS

| | |
|---|---|
| 4 | American Pie |
| 13 | And I Love You So |
| 16 | Angie |
| 22 | Annie's Song |
| 26 | At Seventeen |
| 30 | Blackbird |
| 34 | Don't Let Me Be Lonely Tonight |
| 32 | Dust in the Wind |
| 37 | Fire and Rain |
| 40 | 500 Miles Away from Home |
| 43 | Free Bird |
| 46 | I Will |
| 48 | I'll Follow the Sun |
| 50 | I'm Looking Through You |
| 56 | I've Just Seen a Face |
| 58 | If |
| 60 | If I Had a Hammer (The Hammer Song) |
| 53 | Leaving on a Jet Plane |
| 62 | Longer |
| 64 | Maggie May |
| 70 | Me and Bobby McGee |
| 67 | My Sweet Lady |
| 74 | Norwegian Wood (This Bird Has Flown) |
| 82 | Part of the Plan |
| 86 | Please Come to Boston |
| 77 | Rocky Mountain High |
| 90 | Rocky Raccoon |
| 92 | Summer Breeze |
| 96 | Sunshine on My Shoulders |
| 98 | Turn! Turn! Turn! (To Everything There Is a Season) |
| 100 | Two of Us |
| 106 | Vincent (Starry Starry Night) |
| 110 | Yesterday |
| 103 | You've Got a Friend |
| 112 | **Registration Guide** |

# American Pie

Registration 2
Rhythm: Rock

Words and Music by
Don McLean

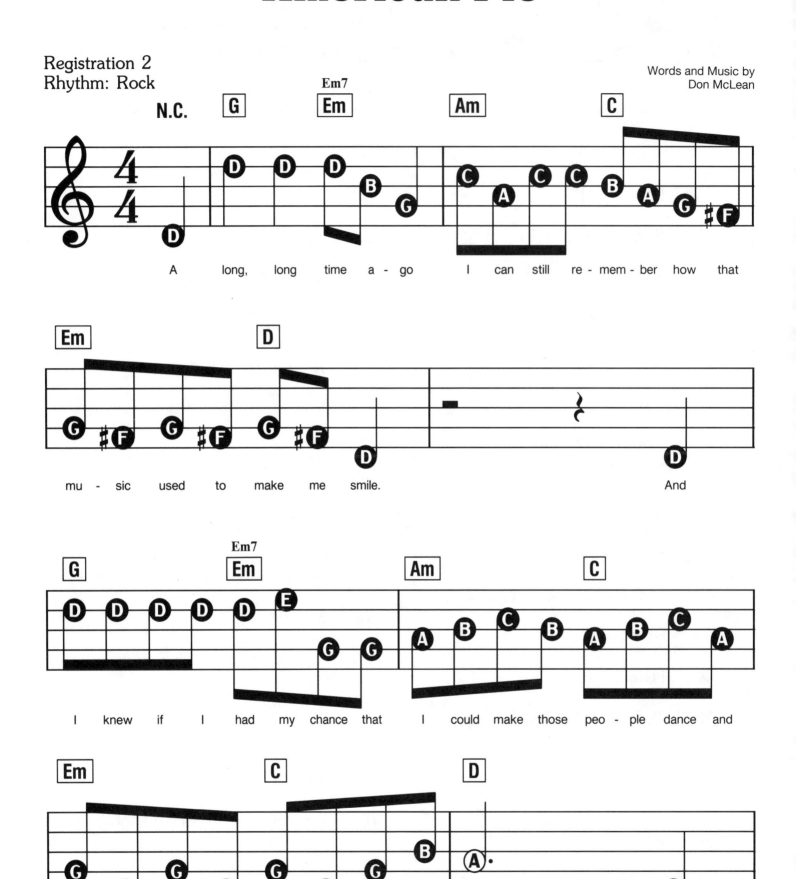

**MCA** music publishing

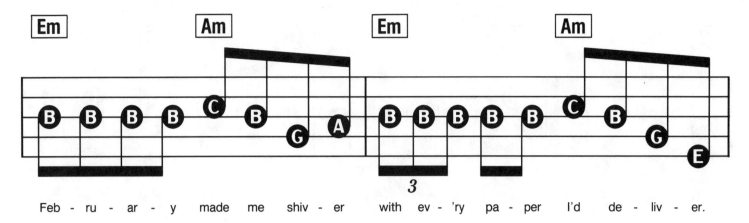

Feb - ru - ar - y made me shiv - er with ev - 'ry pa - per I'd de - liv - er.

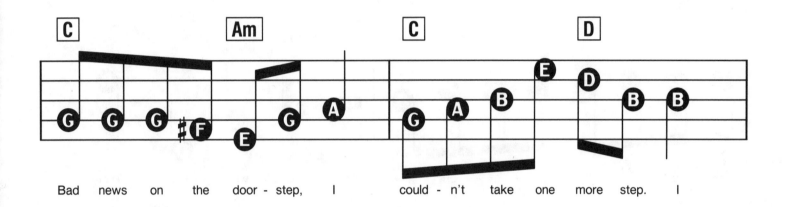

Bad news on the door - step, I could - n't take one more step. I

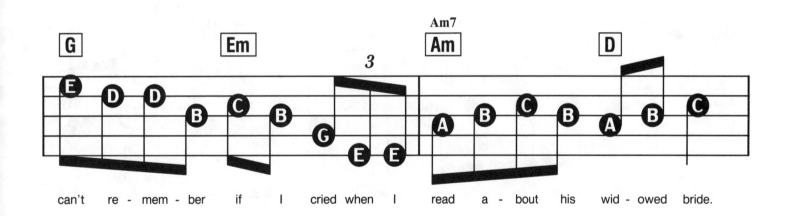

can't re - mem - ber if I cried when I read a - bout his wid - owed bride.

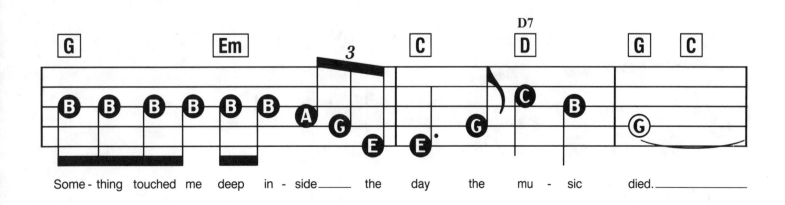

Some - thing touched me deep in - side____ the day the mu - sic died.____

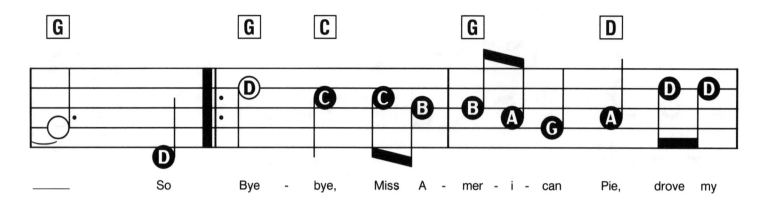

So Bye - bye, Miss A - mer - i - can Pie, drove my

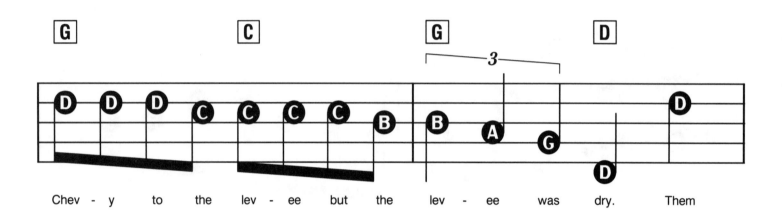

Chev - y to the lev - ee but the lev - ee was dry. Them

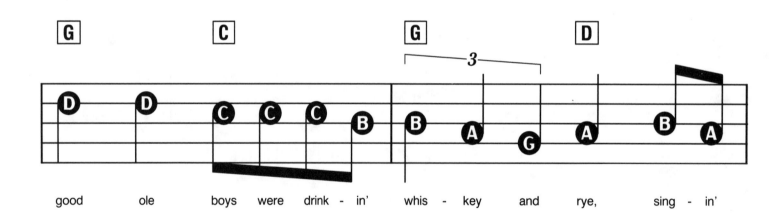

good ole boys were drink - in' whis - key and rye, sing - in'

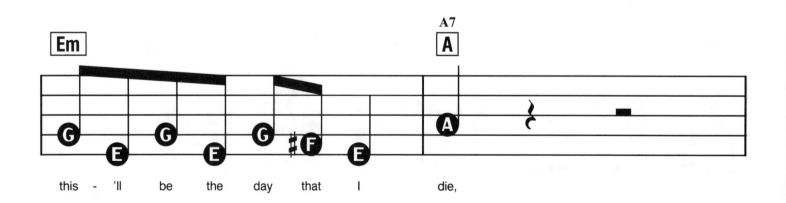

this - 'll be the day that I die,

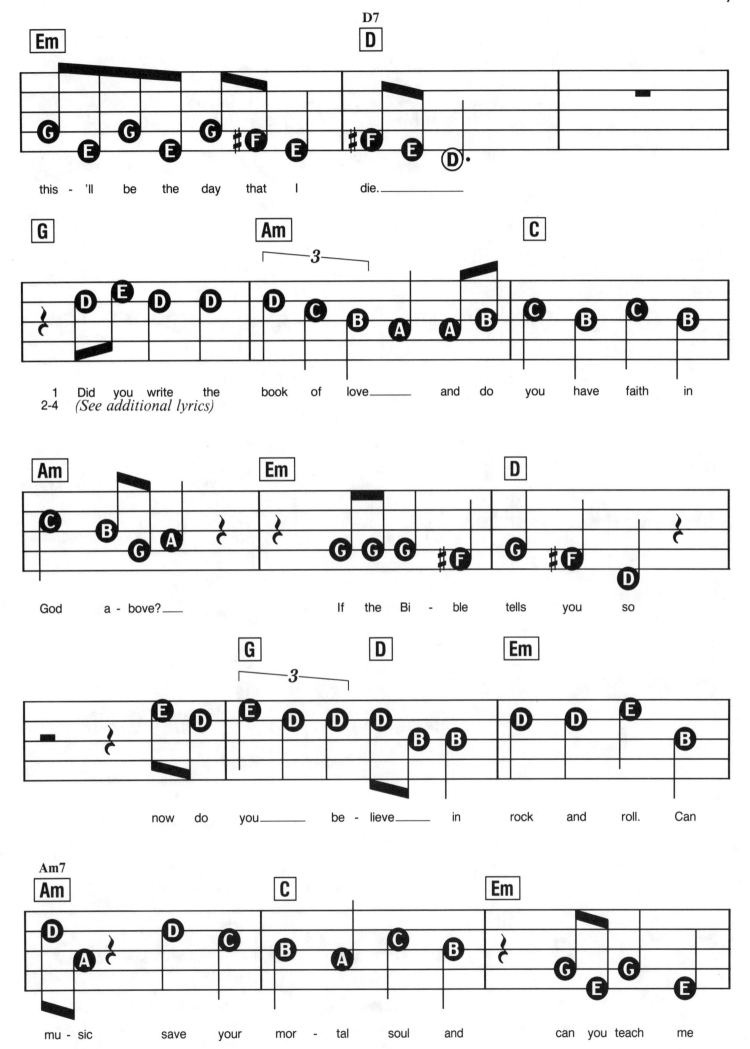

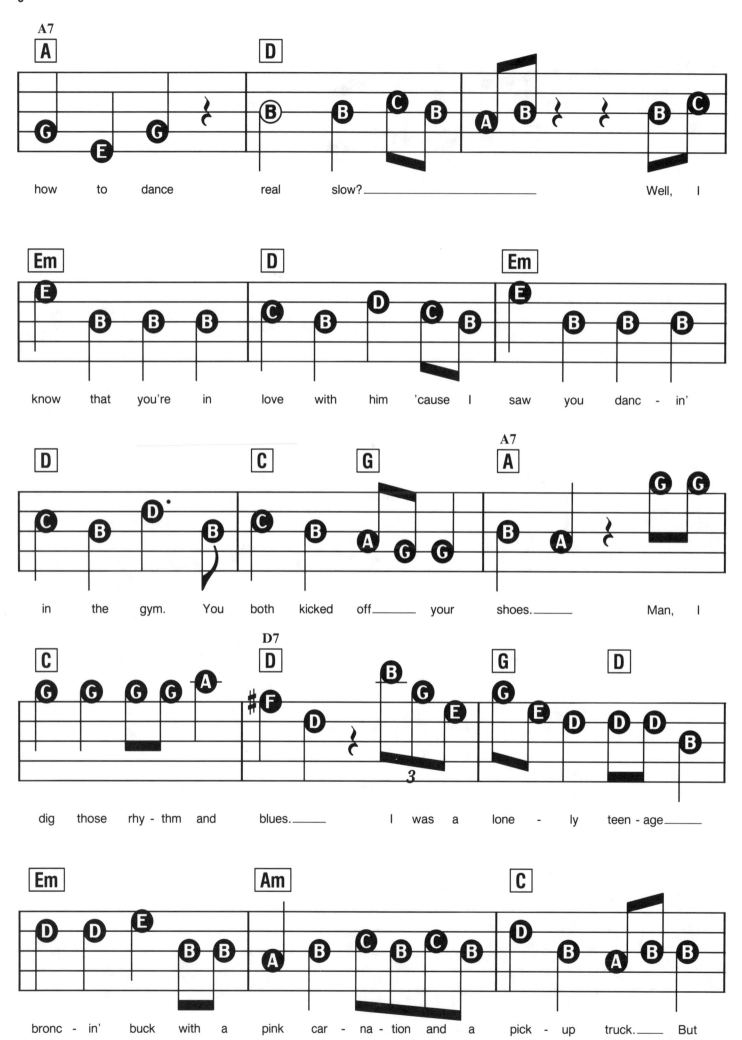

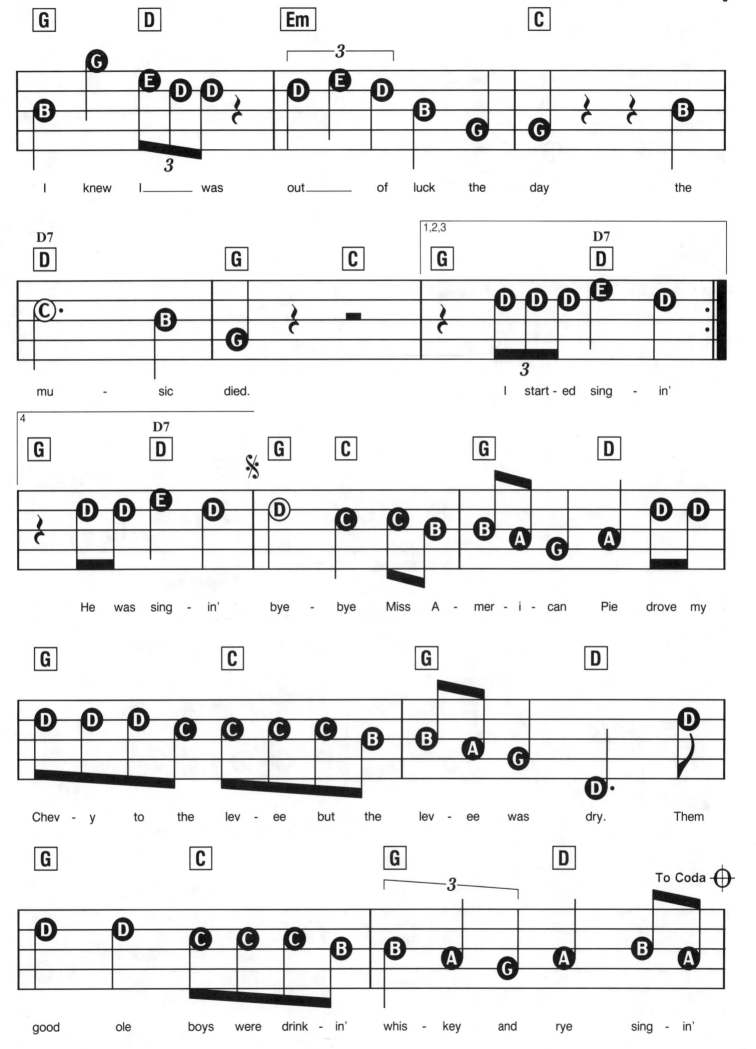

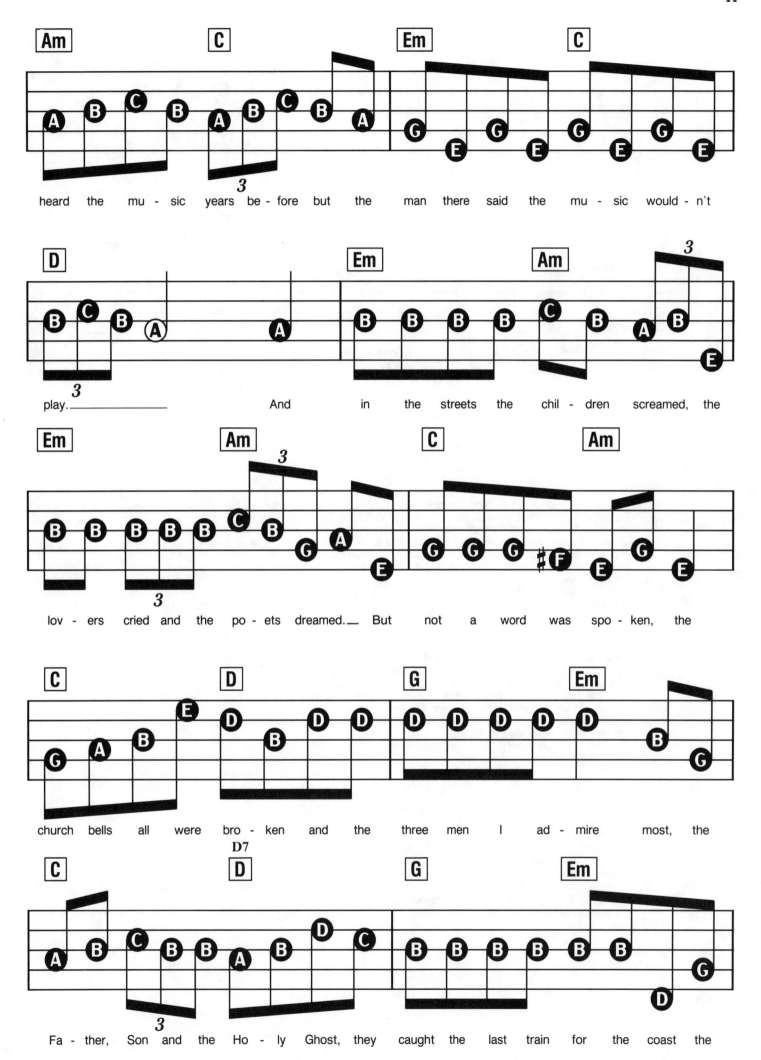

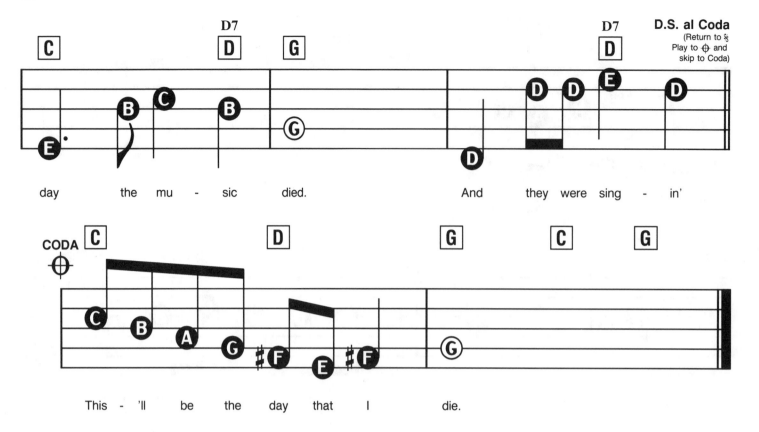

day  the  mu - sic  died.  And  they  were  sing - in'

This - 'll  be  the  day  that  I  die.

## Additional Lyrics

2. Now for ten years we've been on our own, and moss grows fat on a rollin' stone
But that's not how it used to be when the jester sang for the king and queen
In a coat he borrowed from James Dean and a voice that came from you and me
Oh and while the king was looking down, the jester stole his thorny crown
The courtroom was adjourned, no verdict was returned
And while Lenin read a book on Marx the quartet practiced in the park
And we sang dirges in the dark
The day the music died
We were singin'. . . bye-bye. . .,*etc.*

3. Helter-skelter in the summer swelter the birds flew off with a fallout shelter
Eight miles high and fallin' fast, it landed foul on the grass
The players tried for a forward pass, with the jester on the sidelines in a cast
Now the half-time air was sweet perfume while the sergeants played a marching tune
We all got up to dance but we never got the chance
'Cause the players tried to take the field, the marching band refused to yield
Do you recall what was revealed
The day the music died
We started singin'. . . bye-bye. . .,*etc.*

4. And there we were all in one place, a generation lost in space
With no time left to start again
So come on, Jack be nimble, Jack be quick, Jack Flash sat on a candlestick
'Cause fire is the devil's only friend
And as I watched him on the stage my hands were clenched in fists of rage
No angel born in hell could break that Satan's spell
And as the flames climbed high into the night to light the sacrificial rite
I saw Satan laughing with delight the day the music died.
He was singin'. . . bye-bye. . .,*etc.*

# And I Love You So

Registration 3
Rhythm: Pops, 8 Beat, or Bossa Nova

Words and Music by
Don McLean

MCA music publishing

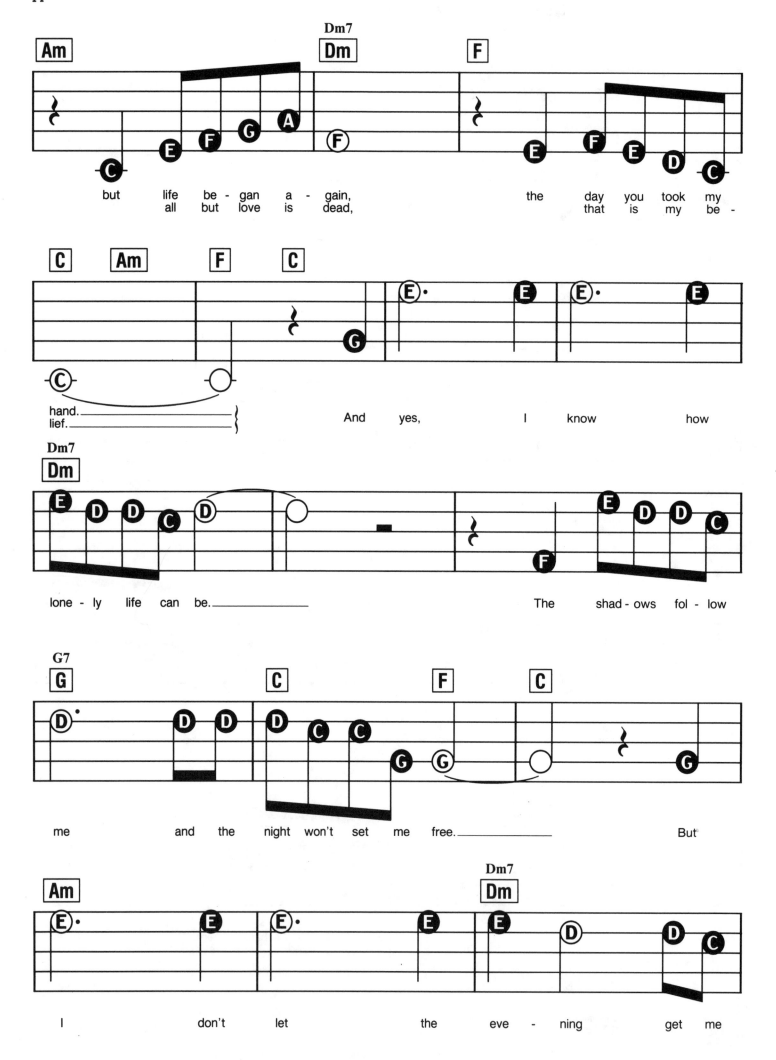

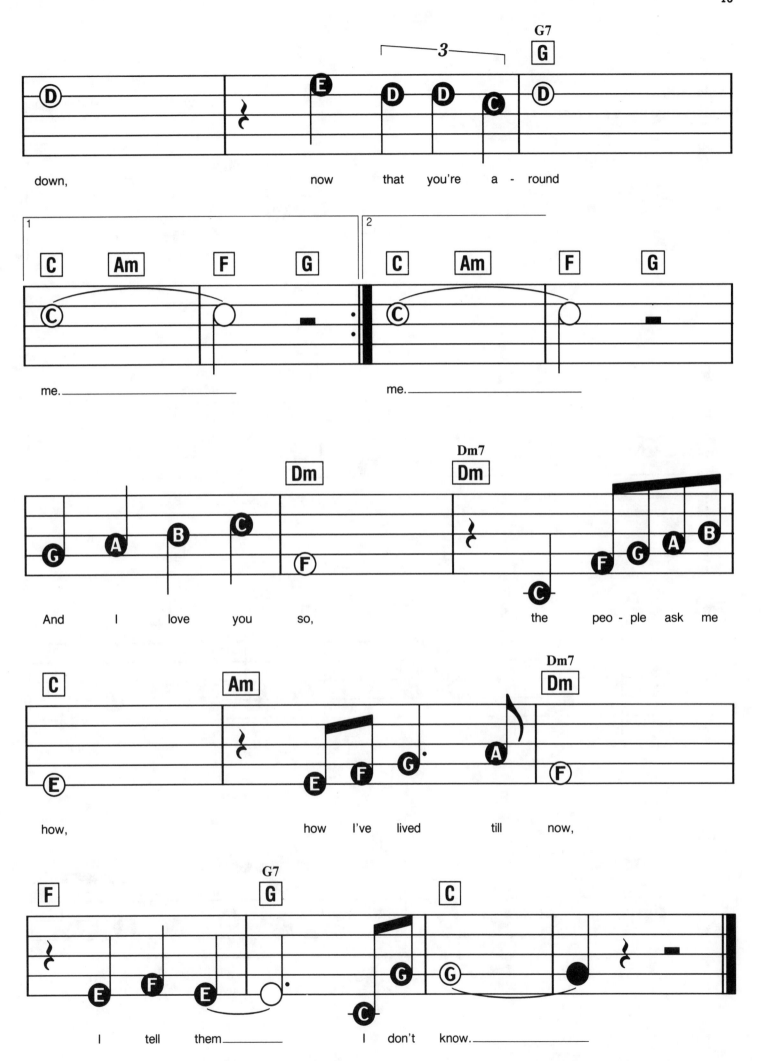

# Angie

Registration 3
Rhythm: Rock or 8 Beat

Words and Music by Mick Jagger
and Keith Richards

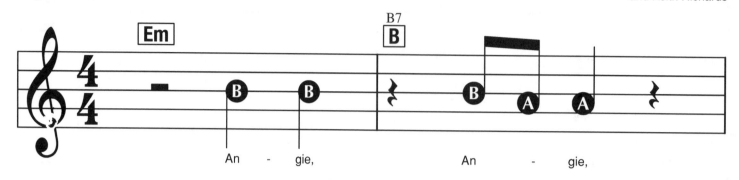

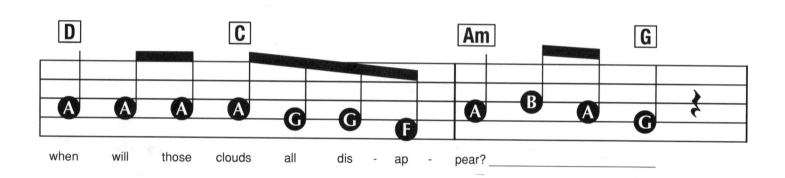

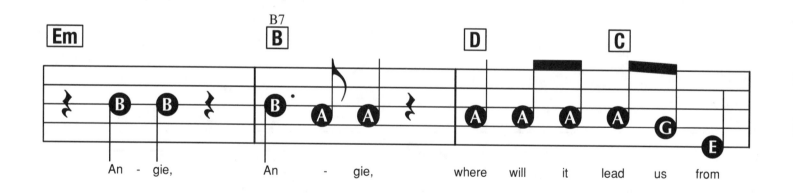

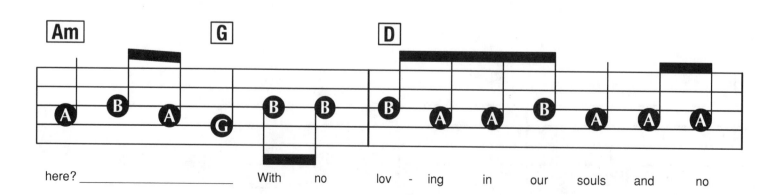

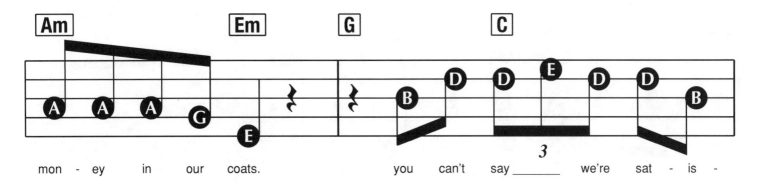

money in our coats. you can't say _____ we're sat - is -

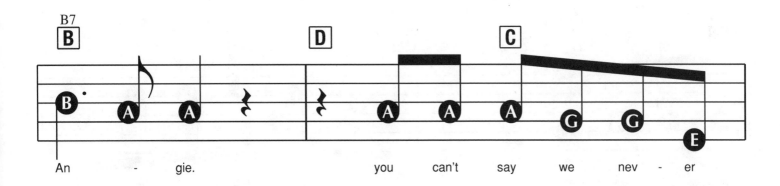

fied. _____ but An - gie.

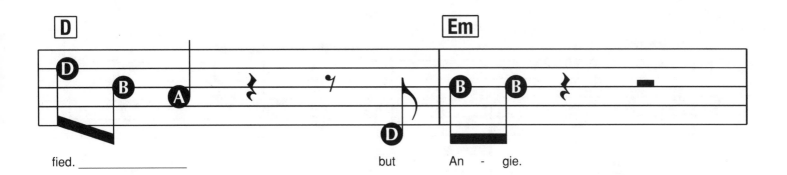

An - gie. you can't say we nev - er

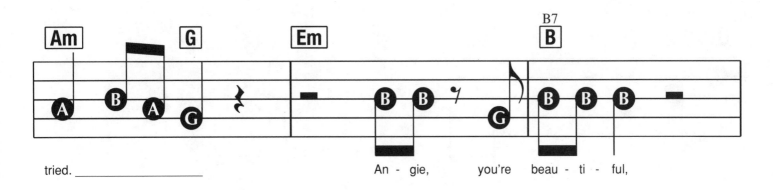

tried. _____ An - gie, you're beau - ti - ful,

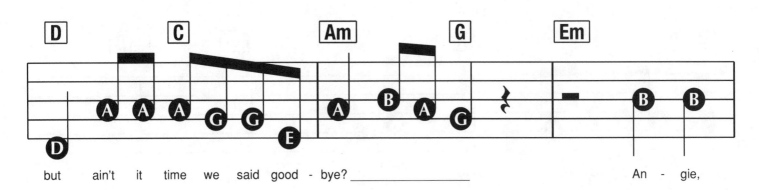

but ain't it time we said good - bye? _____ An - gie,

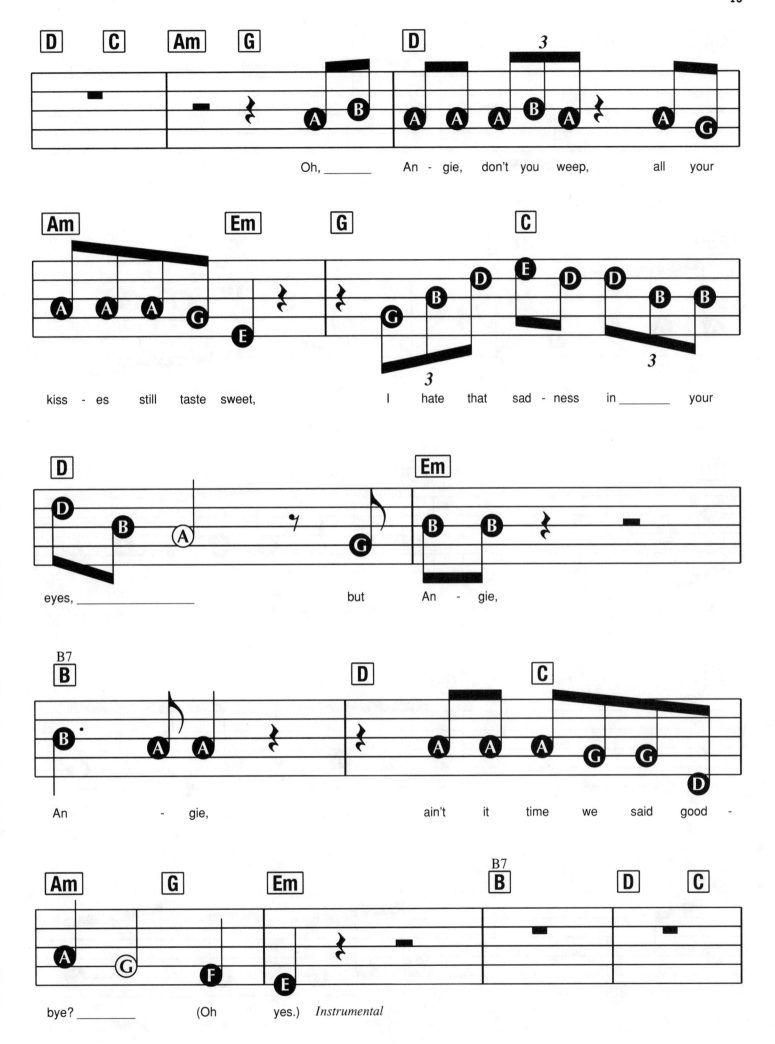

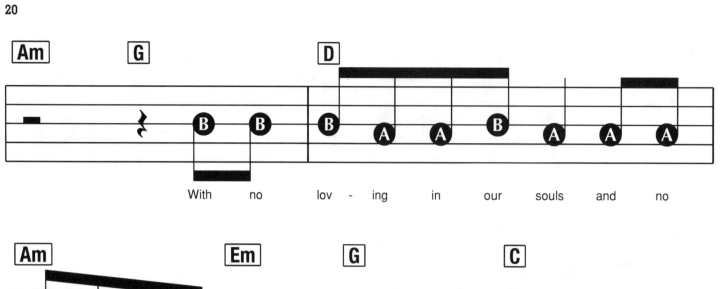

With no lov - ing in our souls and no

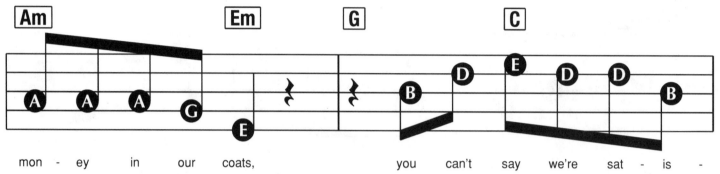

mon - ey in our coats, you can't say we're sat - is -

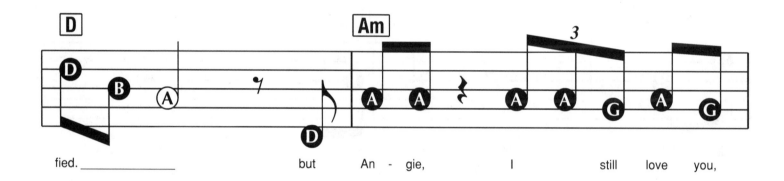

fied. _____ but An - gie, I still love you,

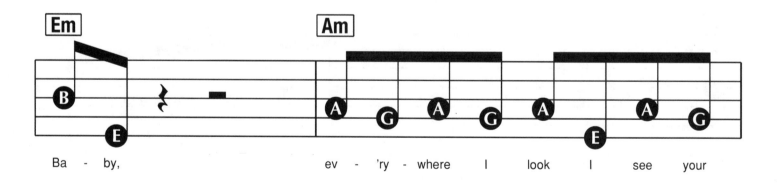

Ba - by, ev - 'ry - where I look I see your

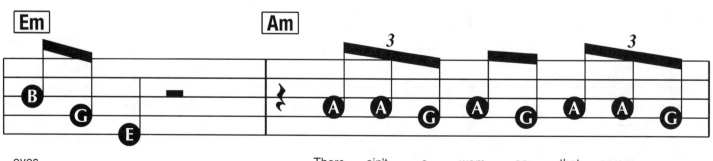

eyes. _____ There ain't a wom - an that comes _____

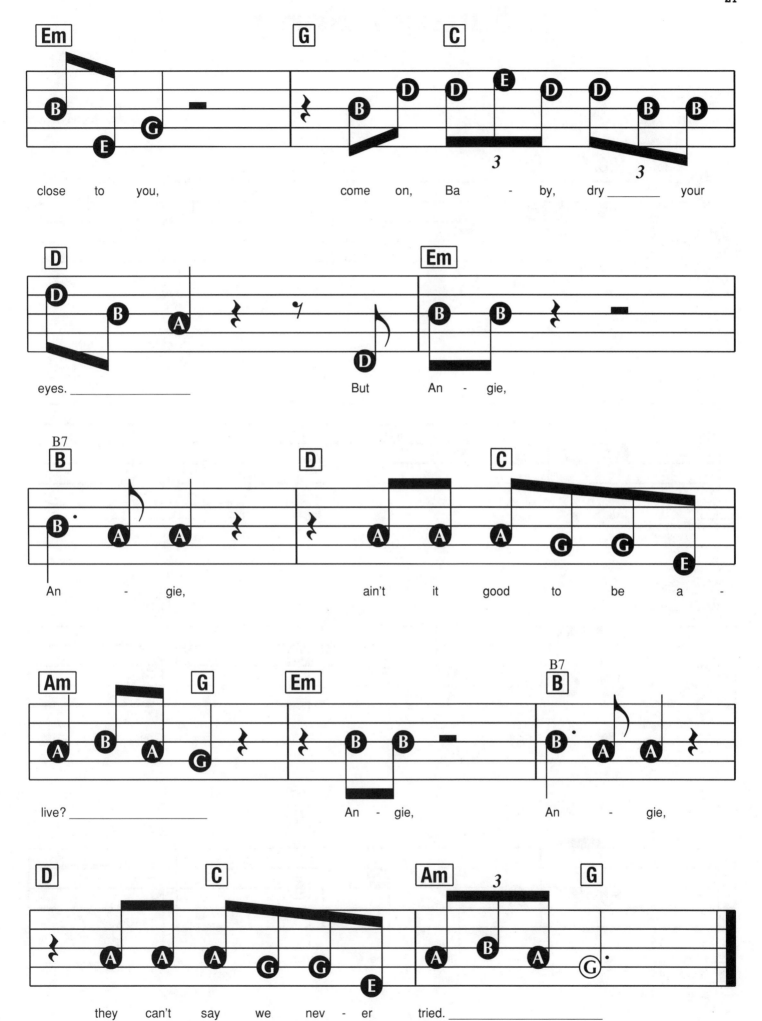

# Annie's Song

Registration 1
Rhythm: Waltz

Words and Music by
John Denver

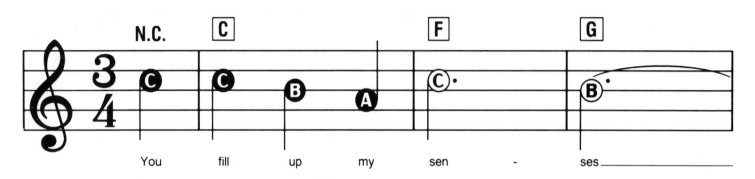

You fill up my sen - ses _____

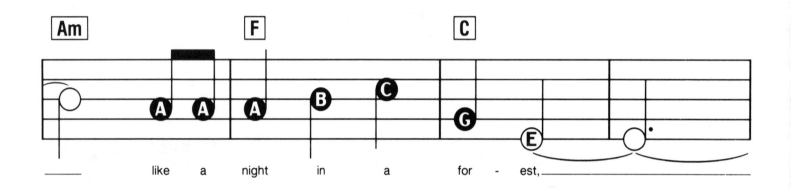

_____ like a night in a for - est, _____

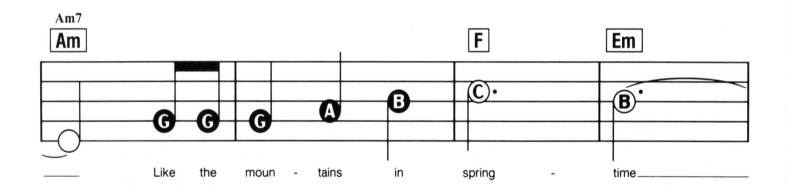

_____ Like the moun - tains in spring - time _____

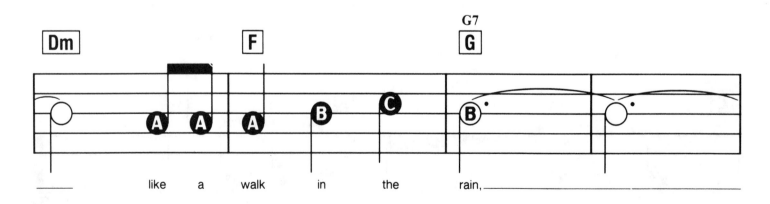

_____ like a walk in the rain, _____

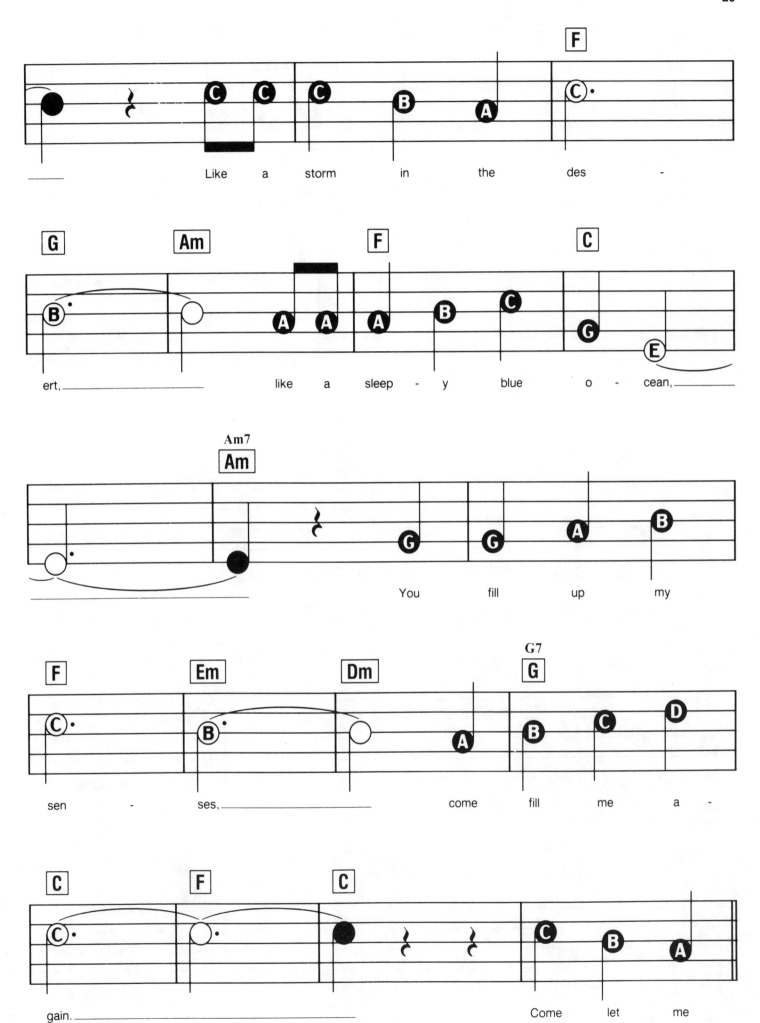

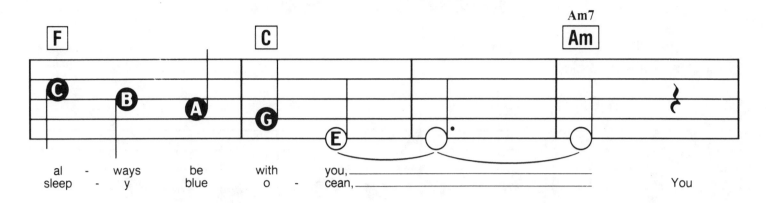

al - ways be with you,_____ You
sleep - y blue o - cean,_____ You

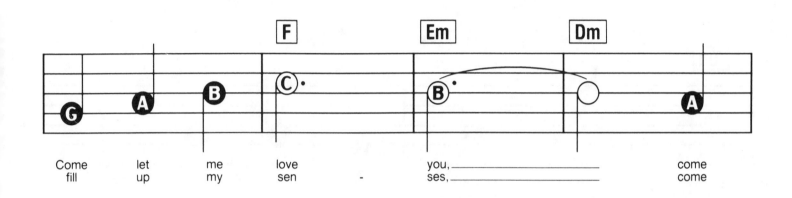

Come let me love you,_____ come
fill up my sen - ses,_____ come

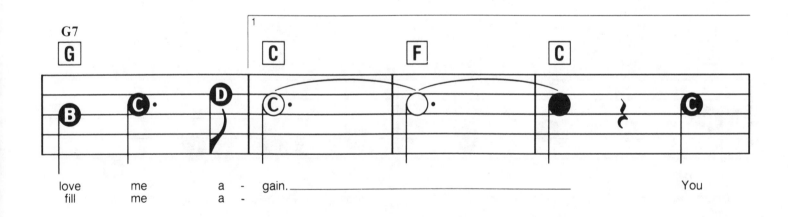

love me a - gain._____ You
fill me a -

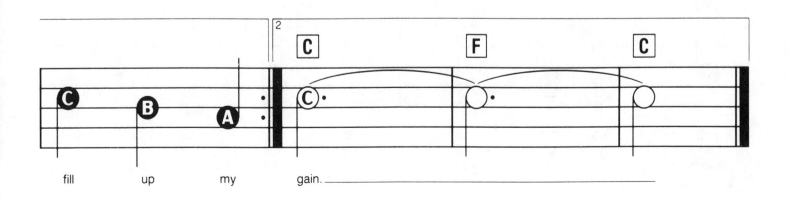

fill up my gain._____

# At Seventeen

Registration 4
Rhythm: Rock or 8 Beat

Words and Music by
Janis Ian

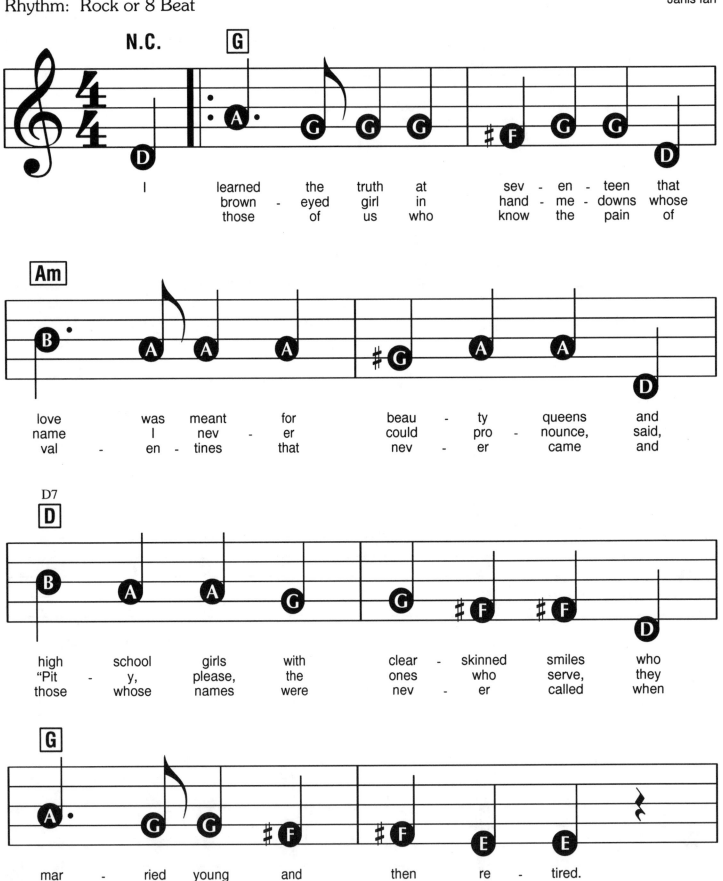

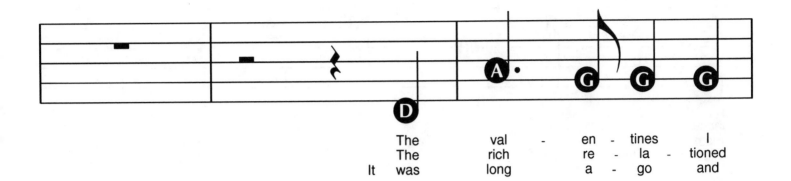

The     val - en - tines   I
The     rich   re - la - tioned
It was   long   a - go   and

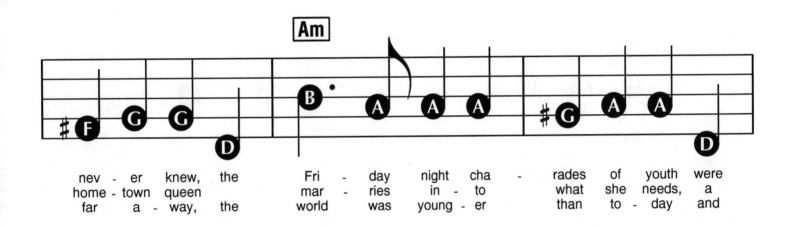

nev - er   knew,   the   Fri - day  night  cha - rades  of  youth  were
home - town queen   the   mar - ries  in - to   what  she  needs,  a
far   a - way,   the   world  was  young - er   than  to - day  and

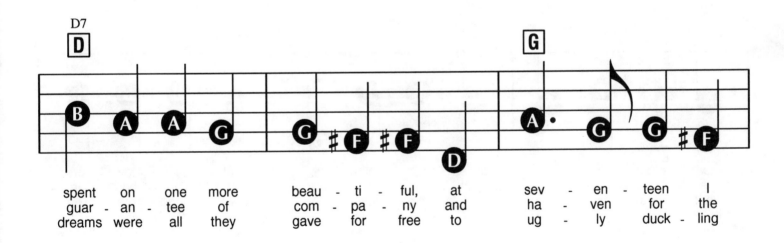

spent  on   one  more   beau - ti - ful,  at   sev - en - teen  I
guar - an - tee  of   com - pa - ny  and   ha - ven  for  the
dreams were   all  they   gave  for  free  to   ug - ly  duck - ling

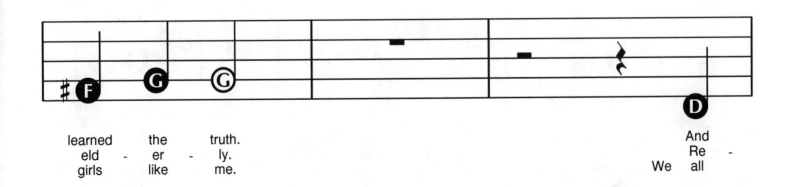

learned  the   truth.                       And
eld - er - ly.                        Re -
girls  like   me.            We  all

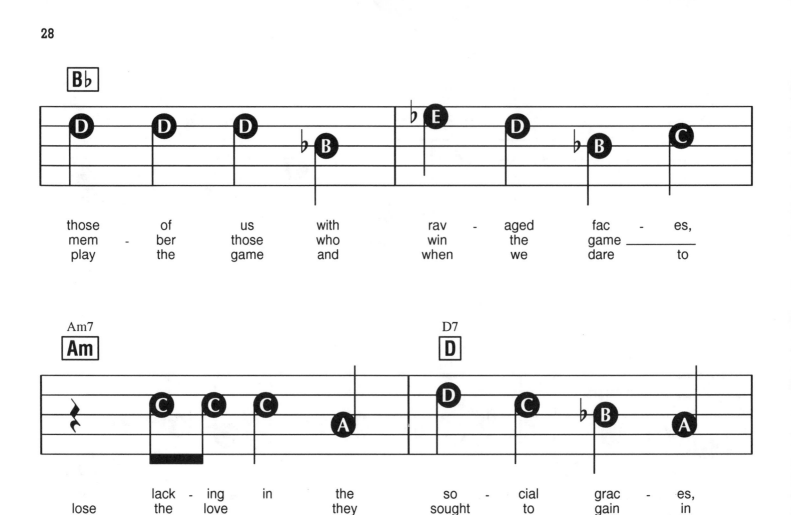

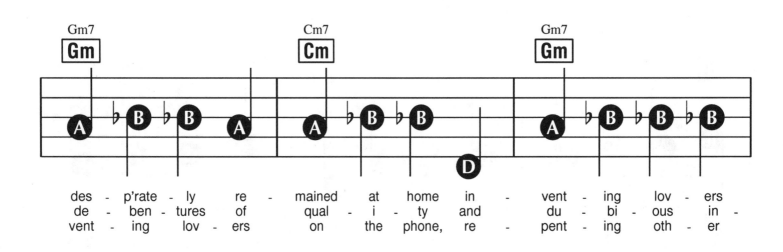

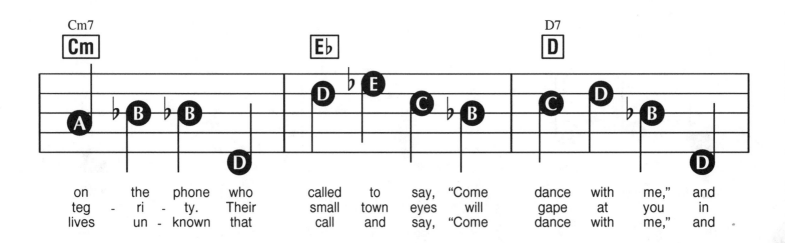

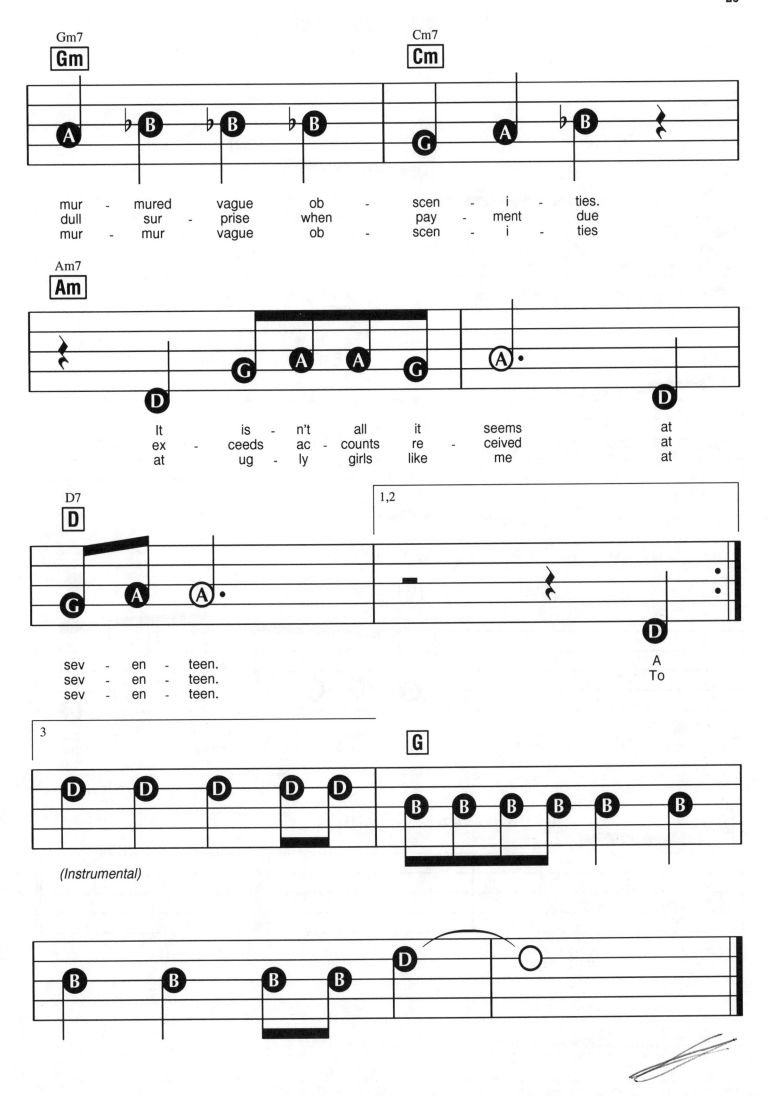

mur - mured vague ob - scen - i - ties.
dull sur - prise when pay - ment due
mur - mur vague ob - scen - i - ties

It is - n't all it seems at
ex - ceeds ac - counts re - ceived at
at ug - ly girls like me at

sev - en - teen.
sev - en - teen.
sev - en - teen.

A
To

(Instrumental)

# Blackbird

Registration 8
Rhythm: Rock

Words and Music by John Lennon
and Paul McCartney

Black - bird sing - ing in the dead of night,
Black - bird sing - ing in the dead of night,

Take these bro - ken wings and learn to fly;
Take these sunk - en eyes and learn to see

All your life you were on - ly wait - ing for this
All your life you were on - ly wait - ing for this

mo - ment to a - rise.
mo - ment to be free.

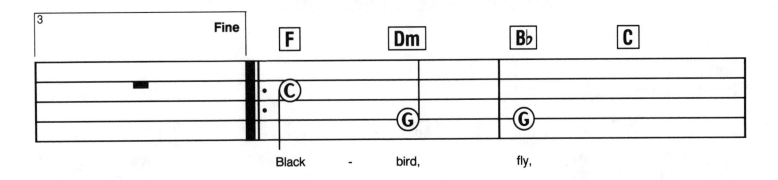

Black - bird, fly,

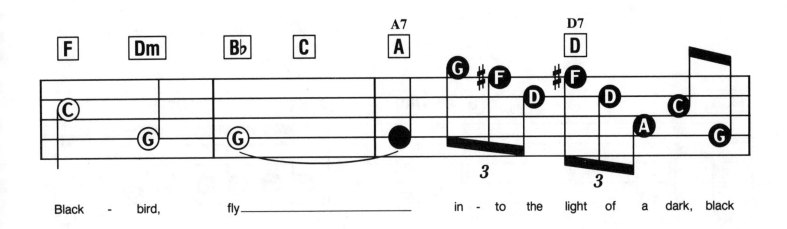

Black - bird, fly_____ in - to the light of a dark, black

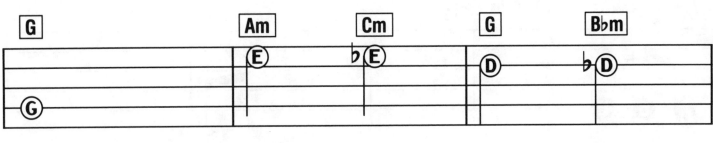

night. *Instrumental*

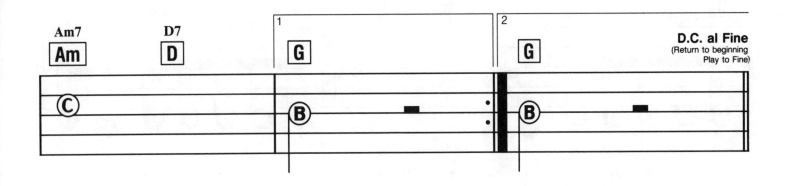

**D.C. al Fine**
(Return to beginning
Play to Fine)

# Dust in the Wind

Registration 10
Rhythm: Rock

Words and Music by
Kerry Livgren

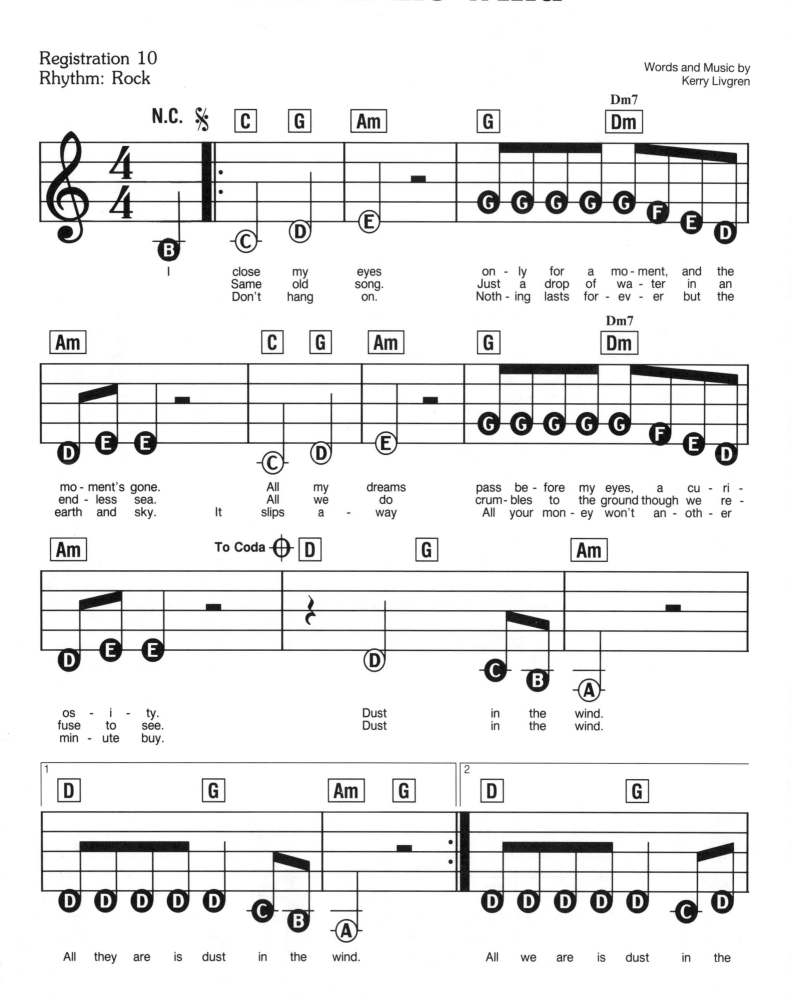

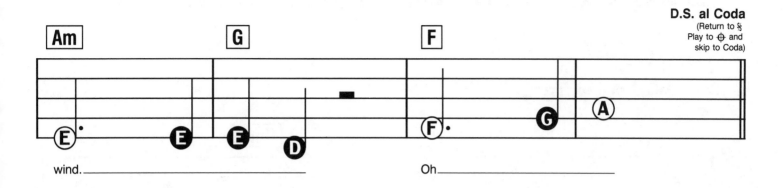

D.S. al Coda
(Return to %
Play to ⊕ and
skip to Coda)

wind. _____ Oh _____

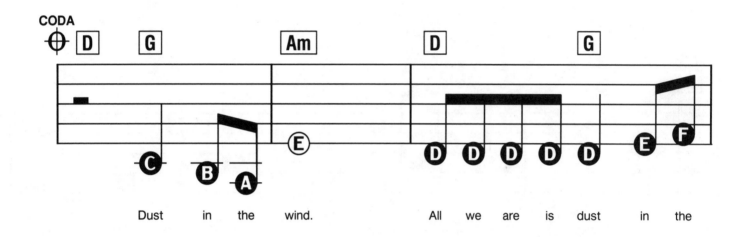

Dust    in    the    wind.    All    we    are    is    dust    in    the

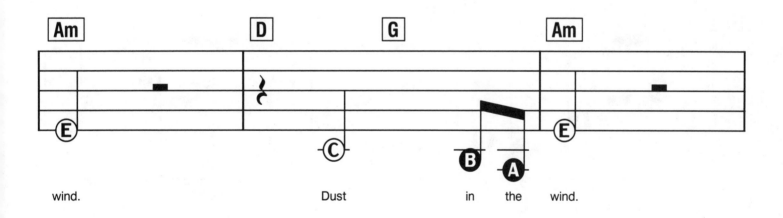

wind.    Dust    in    the    wind.

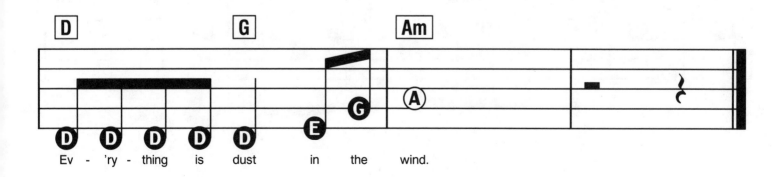

Ev - 'ry - thing    is    dust    in    the    wind.

# Don't Let Me Be Lonely Tonight

Registration 1
Rhythm: Ballad or Fox Trot

Words and Music by
James Taylor

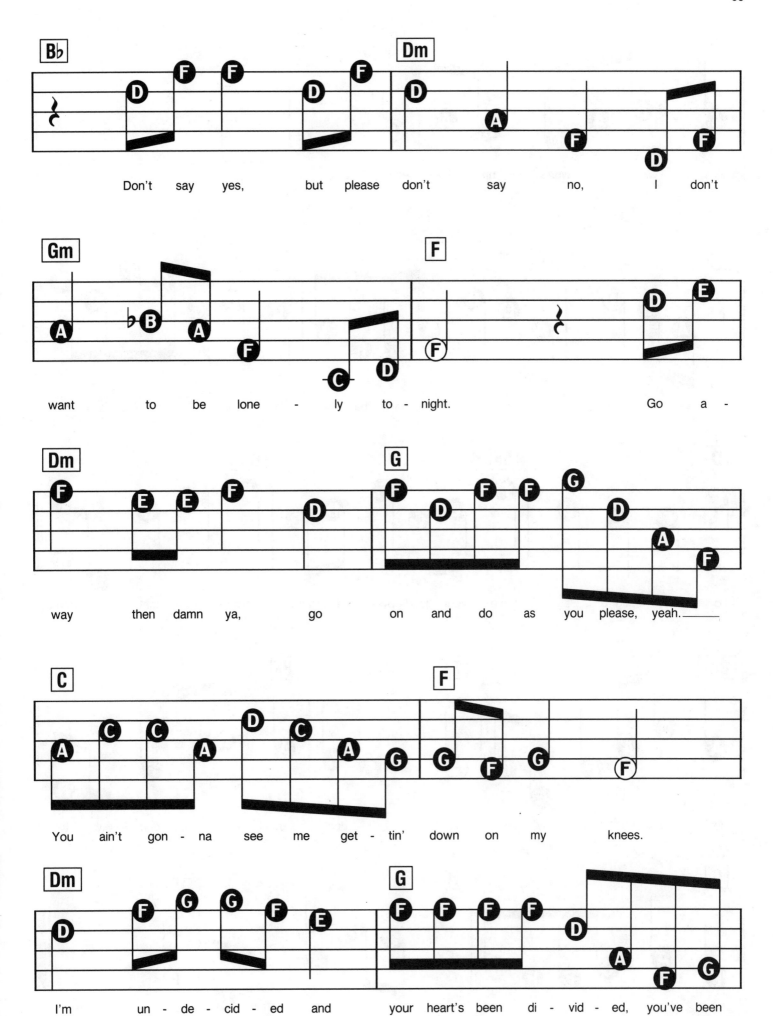

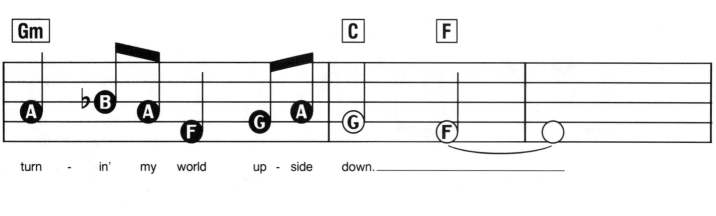

turn - in' my world up - side down._____

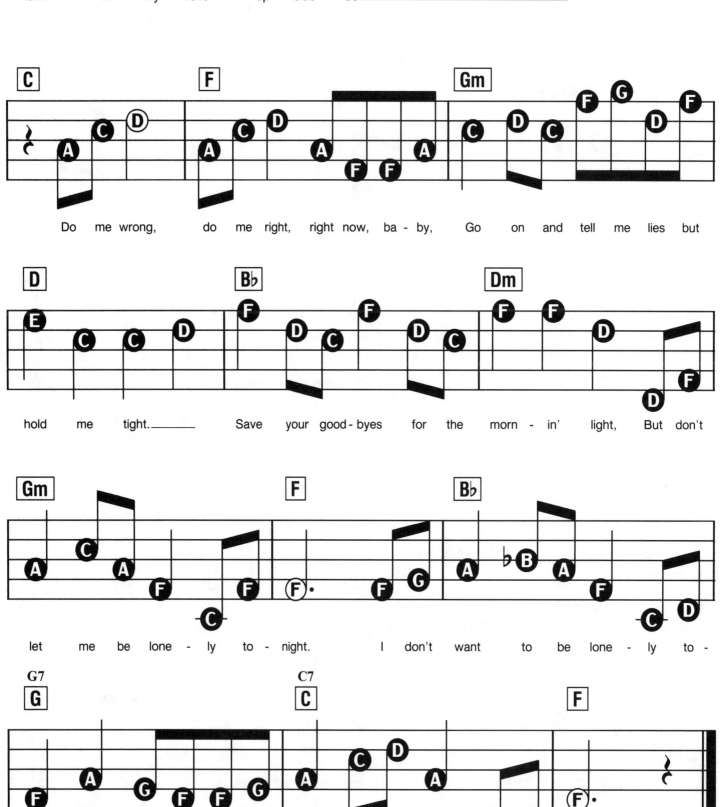

Do me wrong, do me right, right now, ba - by, Go on and tell me lies but

hold me tight._____ Save your good - byes for the morn - in' light, But don't

let me be lone - ly to - night. I don't want to be lone - ly to -

night no, no,_____ I don't want to be lone - ly to - night.

# Fire and Rain

Registration 2
Rhythm: Rock

Words and Music by
James Taylor

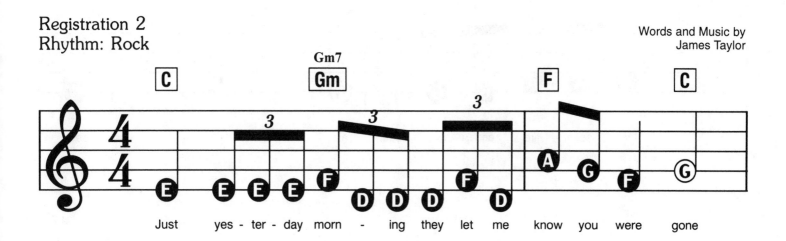

Just yes - ter - day morn - ing they let me know you were gone

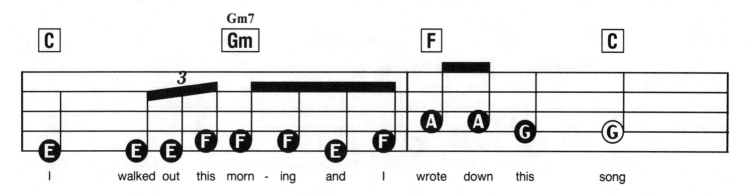

Su - san the plans they made put an end to you

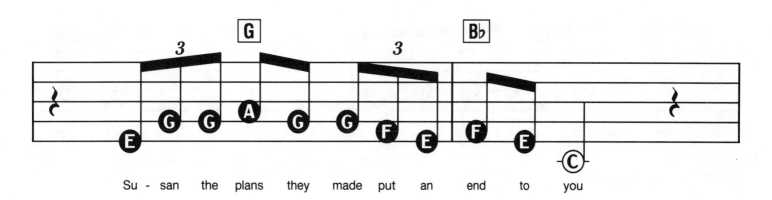

I walked out this morn - ing and I wrote down this song

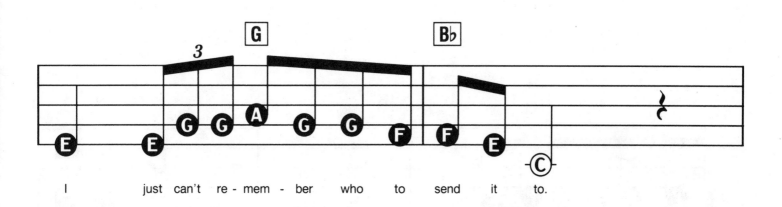

I just can't re - mem - ber who to send it to.

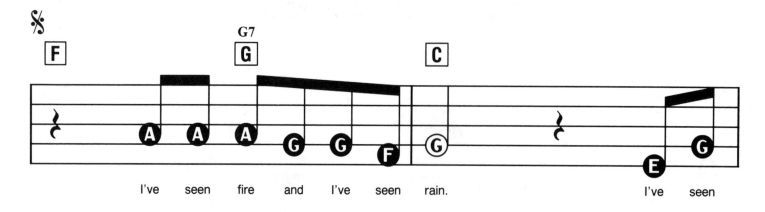

I've seen fire and I've seen rain. I've seen

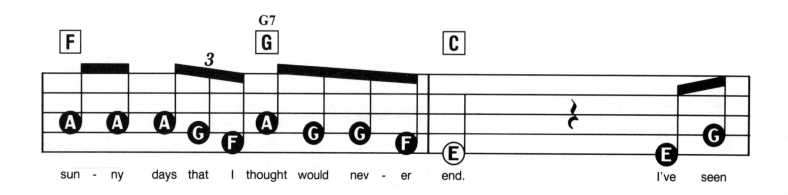

sun - ny days that I thought would nev - er end. I've seen

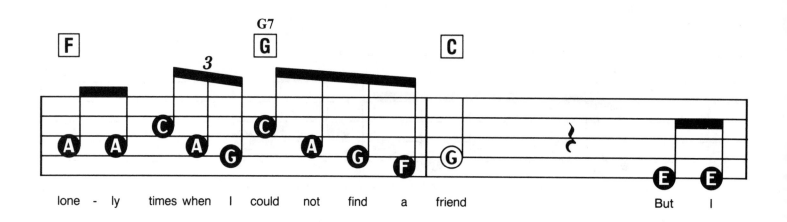

lone - ly times when I could not find a friend But I

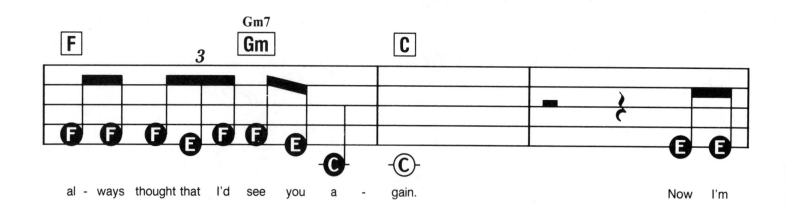

al - ways thought that I'd see you a - gain. Now I'm

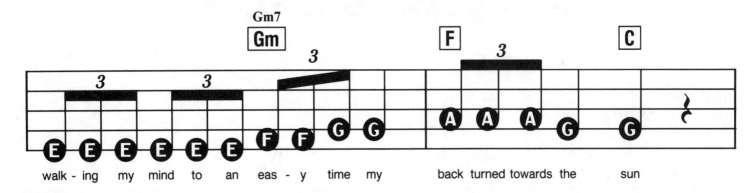

walk - ing my mind to an eas - y time my back turned towards the sun

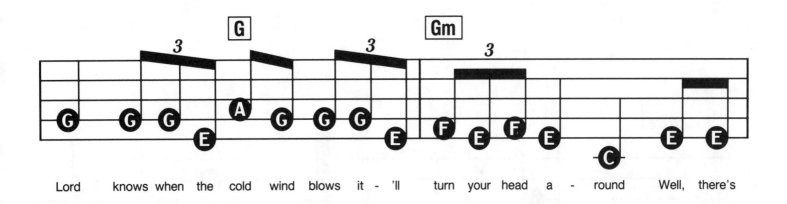

Lord knows when the cold wind blows it - 'll turn your head a - round Well, there's

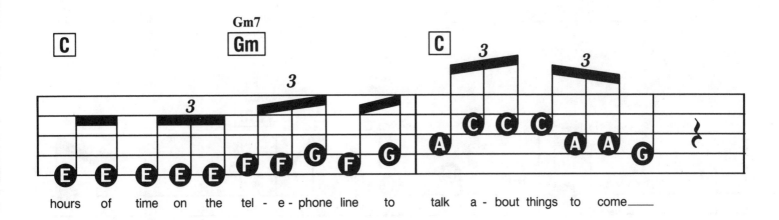

hours of time on the tel - e - phone line to talk a - bout things to come____

**D.S. and Fade**
(Return to 𝄋 and Fade)

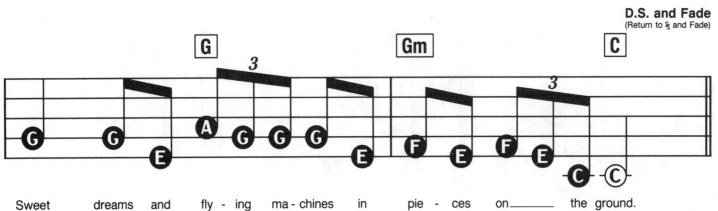

Sweet dreams and fly - ing ma - chines in pie - ces on____ the ground.

# 500 Miles Away from Home

Registration 3
Rhythm: Fox Trot

Words and Music by Bobby Bare,
Charlie Williams and Hedy West

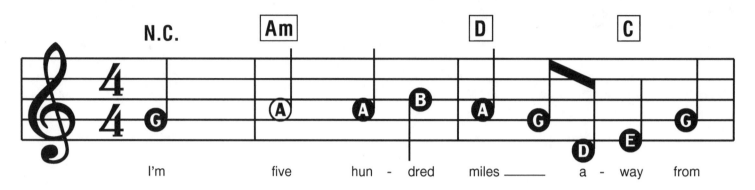

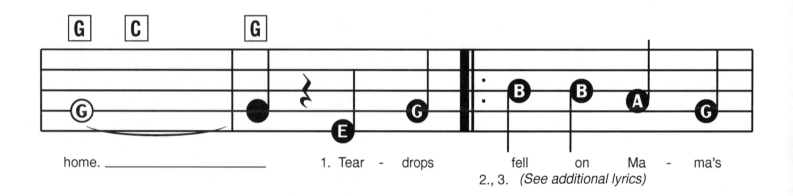

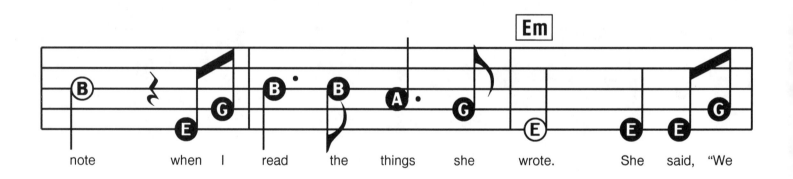

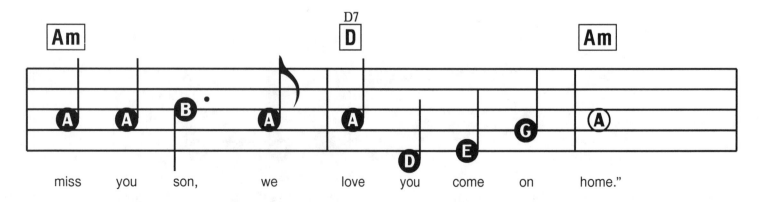

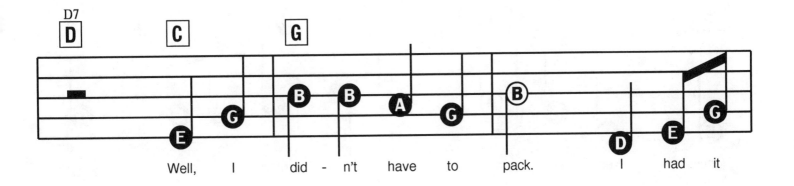

Well, I did-n't have to pack. I had it

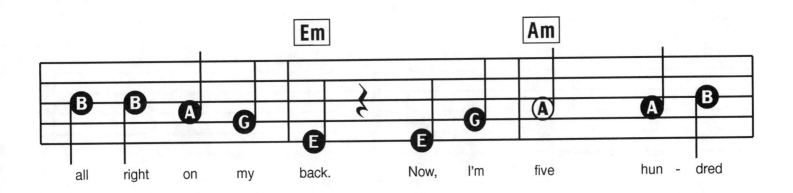

all right on my back. Now, I'm five hun-dred

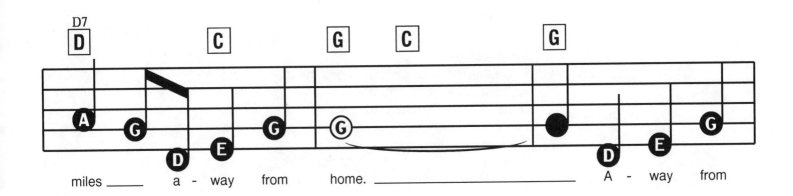

miles _____ a-way from home. _____ A-way from

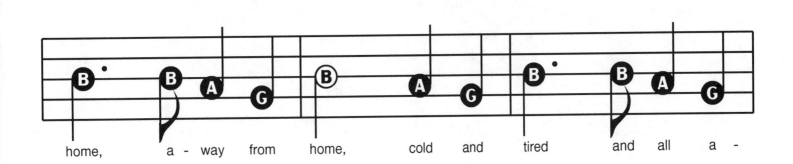

home, a-way from home, cold and tired and all a-

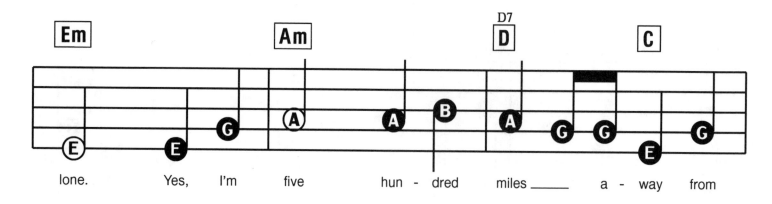

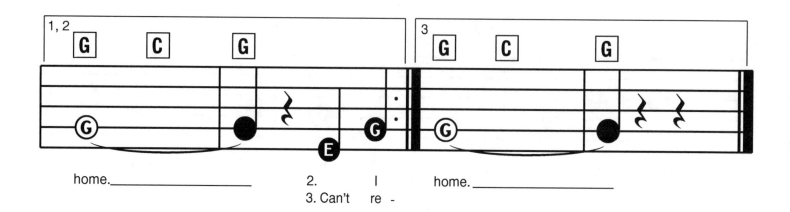

### Additional Lyrics

2. *(Recitation over music)*
   I know this is the same road I took the day I left home,
   But it sure looks different now.
   I guess I look different, too,
   'cause time changes everything.
   I wonder what they'll say
   When they see their boy lookin' this way?
   *(Sung)* I wonder what they'll say when I get home.

3. Can't remember when I ate,
   it's just thumb, walk and wait,
   and I'm still five hundred miles away from home.
   If my luck had been just right
   I'd be with them all tonight,
   But I'm still five hundred miles away from home.
   *Chorus:*
   Away from home, away from home,
   cold and tired and all alone,
   yes, I'm still five hundred miles away from home.
   Oh, I'm still five hundred miles away from home.

# Free Bird

Registration 2
Rhythm: Slow Rock or 12 Beat

Words and Music by Allen Collins
and Ronnie Van Zant

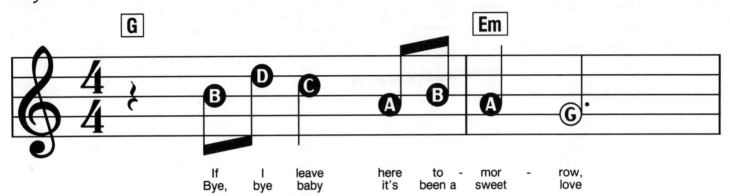

If I leave here to-mor-row,
Bye, bye baby it's been a sweet love

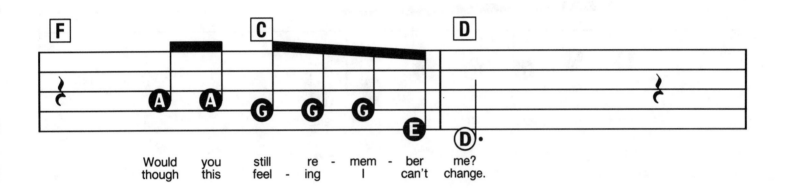

Would you still re-mem-ber me?
though this feel-ing I can't change.

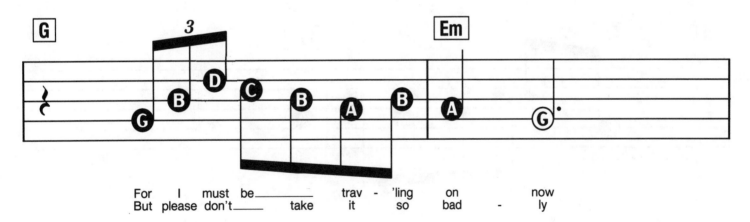

For I must be_____ trav-'ling on now
But please don't_____ take it so bad-ly

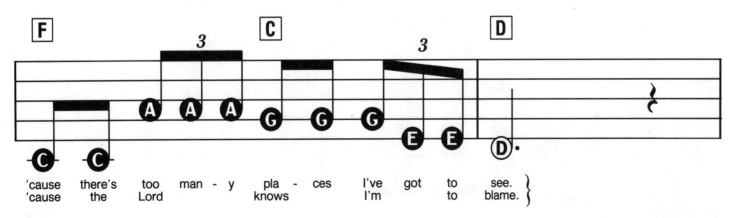

'cause there's too man-y pla-ces I've got to see.
'cause the Lord knows I'm to blame.

**MCA** music publishing

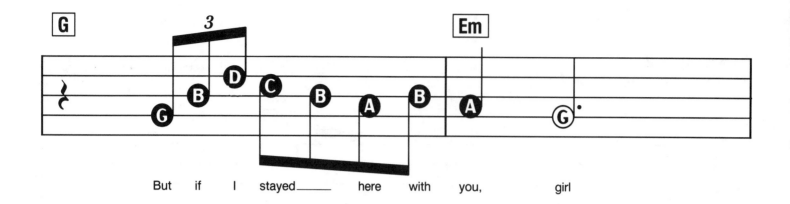

But if I stayed____ here with you, girl

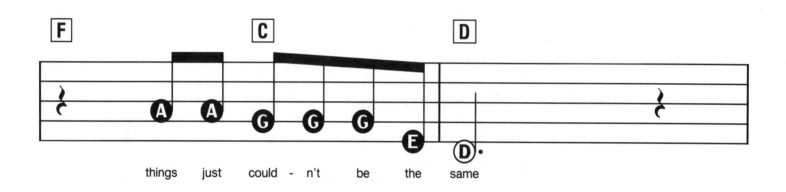

things just could - n't be the same

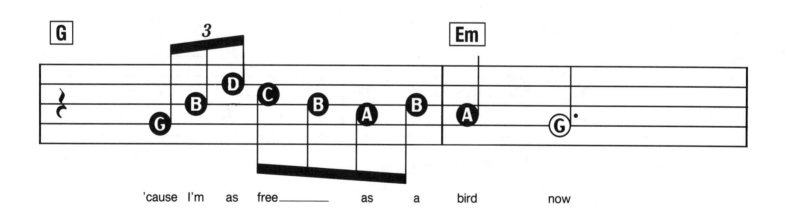

'cause I'm as free____ as a bird now

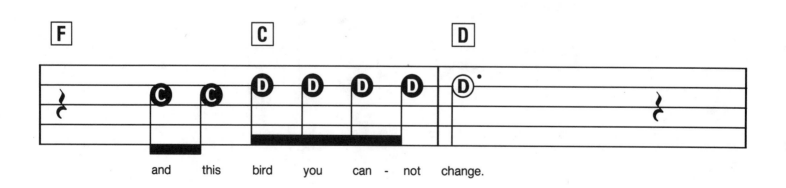

and this bird you can - not change.

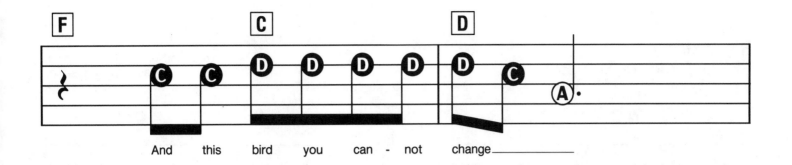

And this bird you can - not change_____

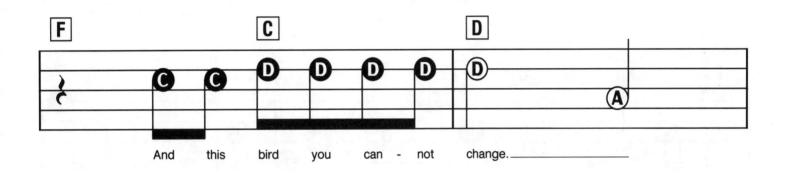

And this bird you can - not change._____

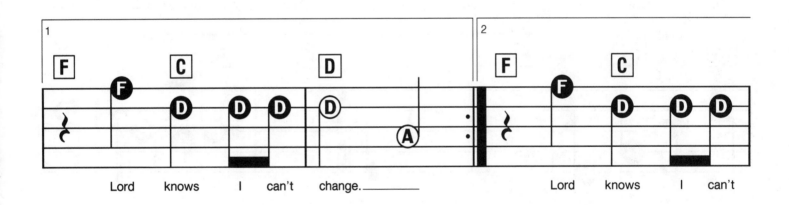

Lord knows I can't change._____ Lord knows I can't

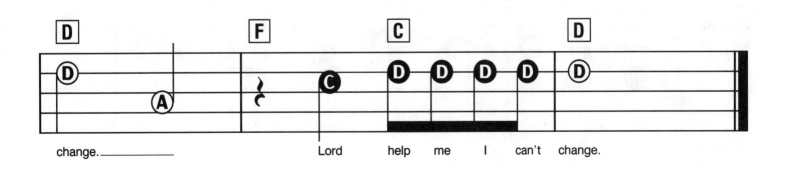

change._____ Lord help me I can't change.

# I Will

Registration 4
Rhythm: Rock or Slow Rock

Words and Music by John Lennon
and Paul McCartney

# I'll Follow the Sun

Registration 7
Rhythm: Rock or Latin

Words and Music by John Lennon
and Paul McCartney

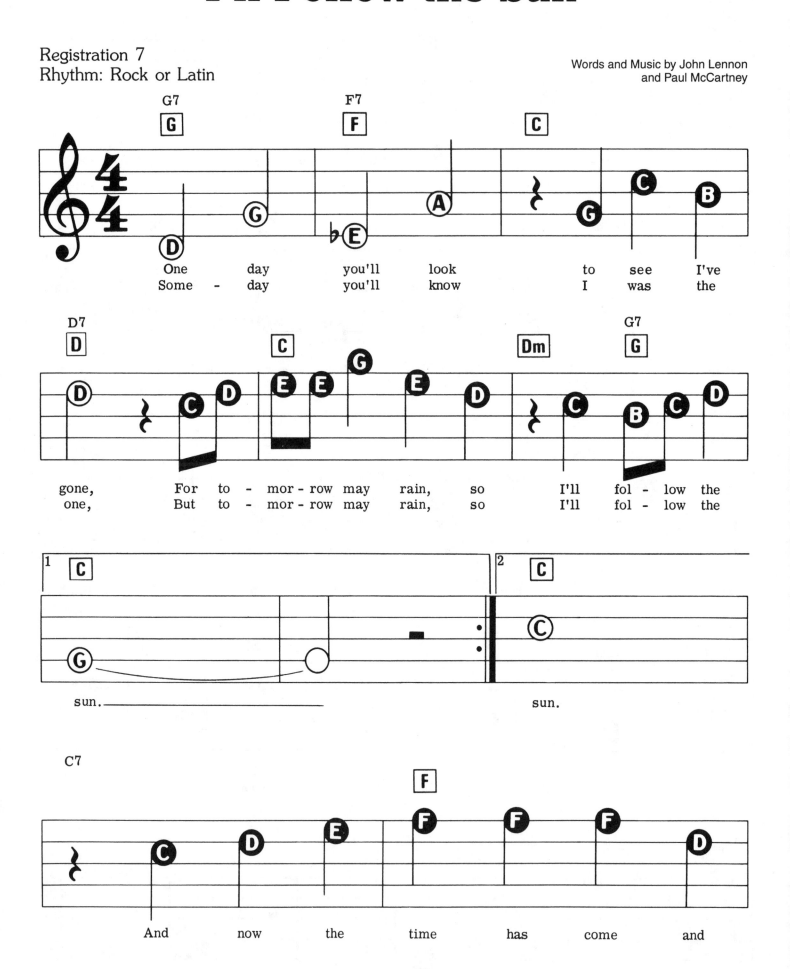

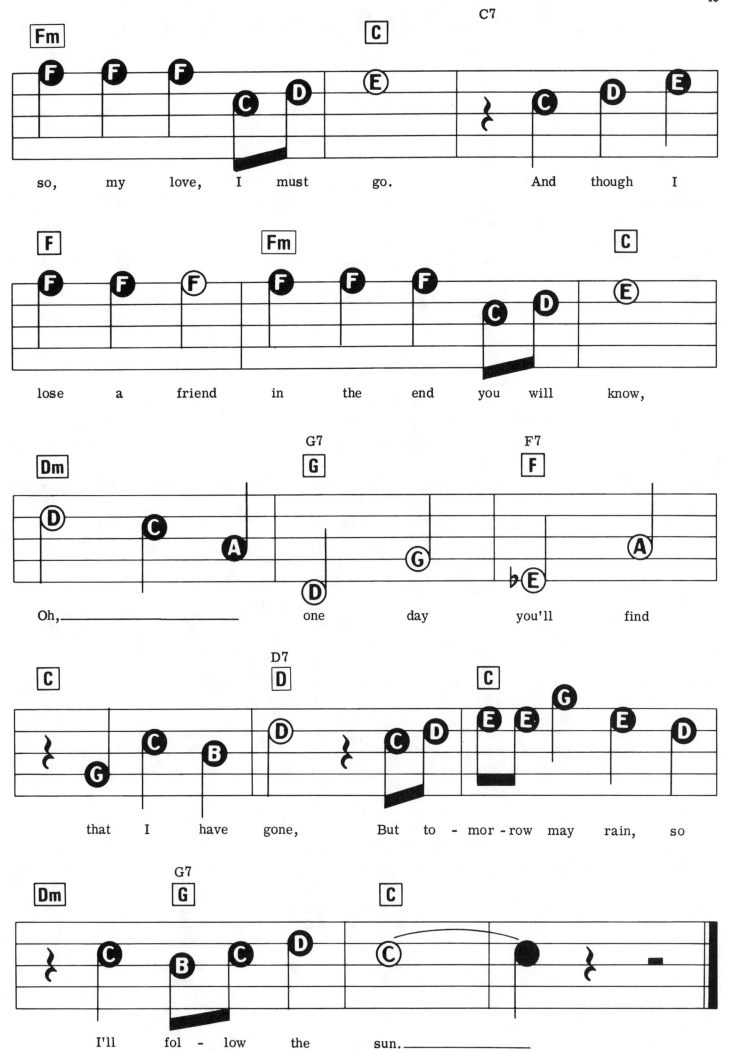

# I'm Looking Through You

Registration 2
Rhythm: Rock or Shuffle

Words and Music by John Lennon
and Paul McCartney

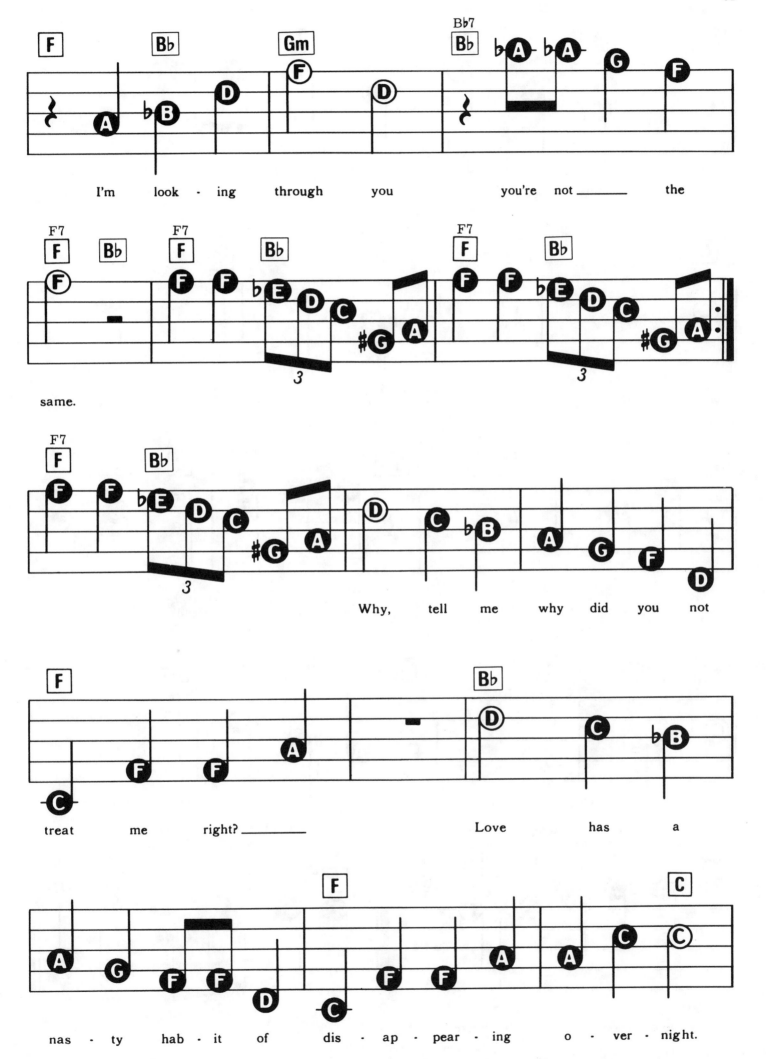

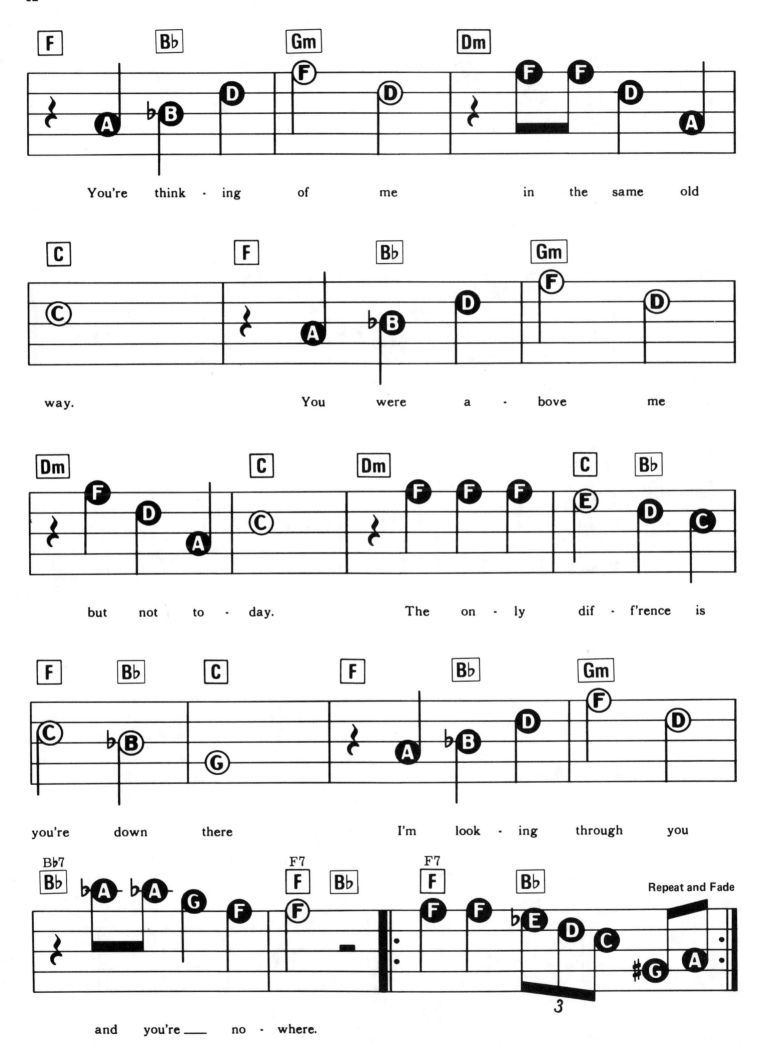

You're think · ing of me in the same old

way. You were a · bove me

but not to · day. The on · ly dif · f'rence is

you're down there I'm look · ing through you

and you're __ no · where.

# Leaving on a Jet Plane

Registration 1
Rhythm: Rock or Slow Rock

Words and Music by
John Denver

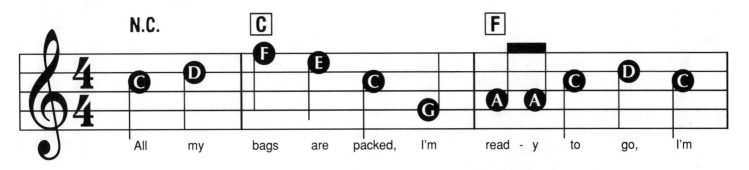

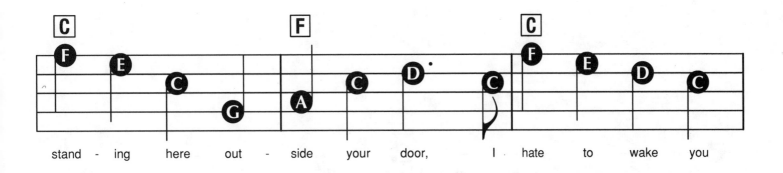

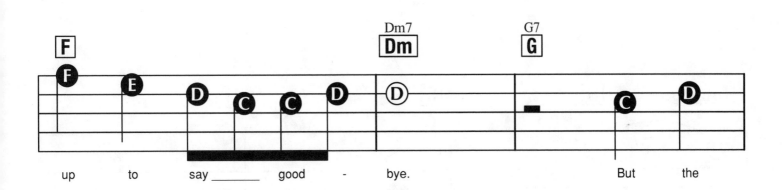

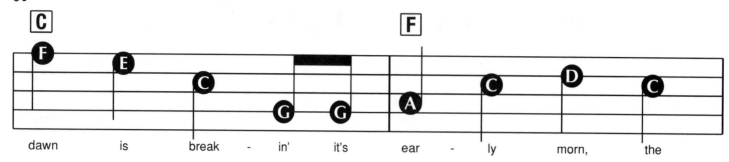

dawn  is  break - in'  it's  ear - ly  morn,  the

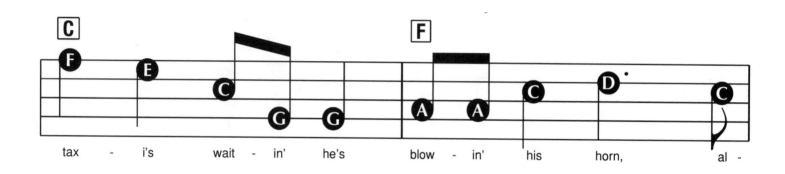

tax - i's  wait - in'  he's  blow - in'  his  horn,  al -

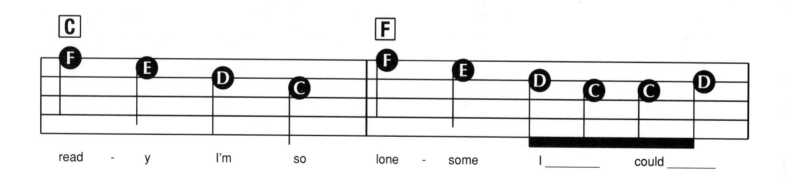

read - y  I'm  so  lone - some  I _____ could _____

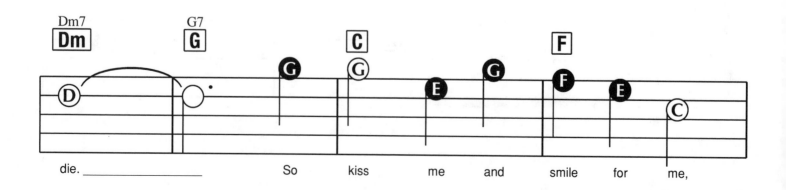

die. _____  So  kiss  me  and  smile  for  me,

55

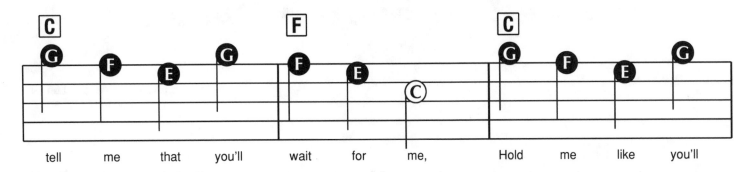

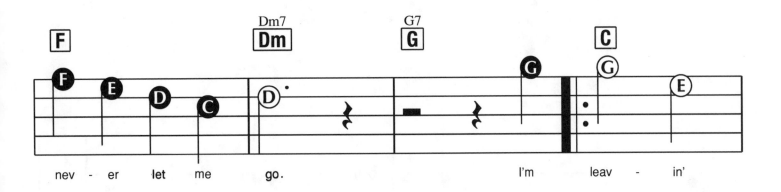

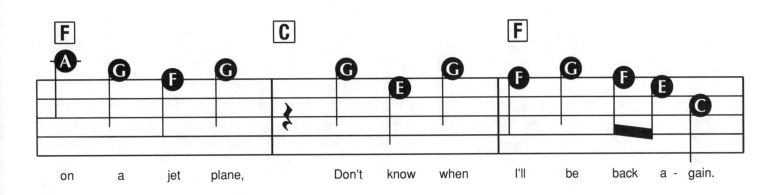

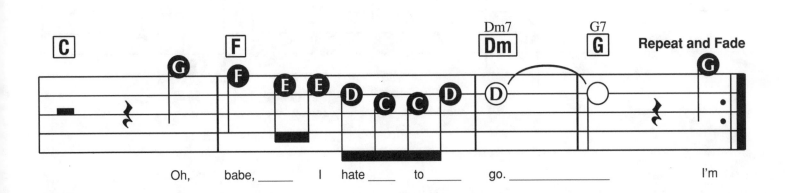

# I've Just Seen a Face

Registration 4
Rhythm: Rock

Words and Music by John Lennon
and Paul McCartney

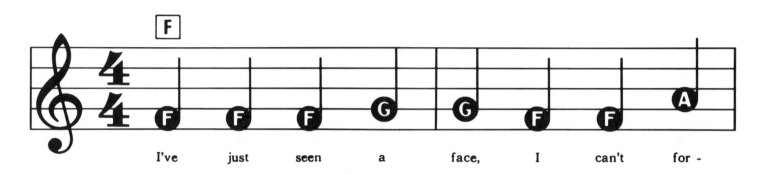

I've just seen a face, I can't for -

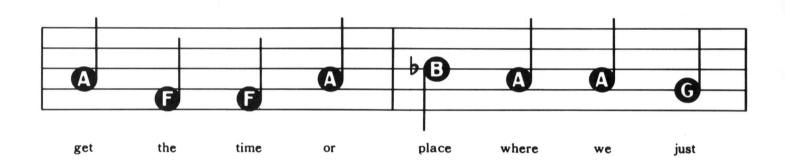

get the time or place where we just

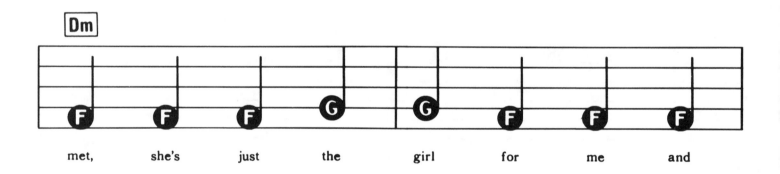

met, she's just the girl for me and

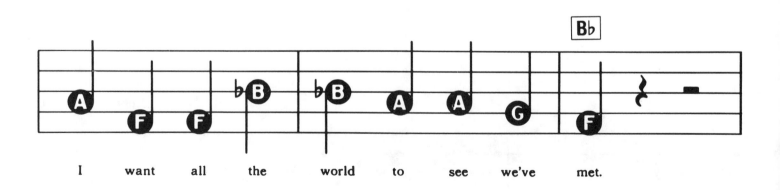

I want all the world to see we've met.

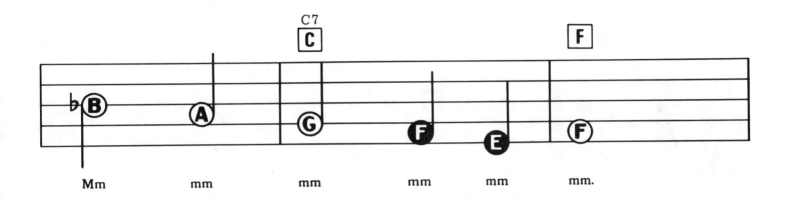

Mm    mm    mm    mm    mm    mm.

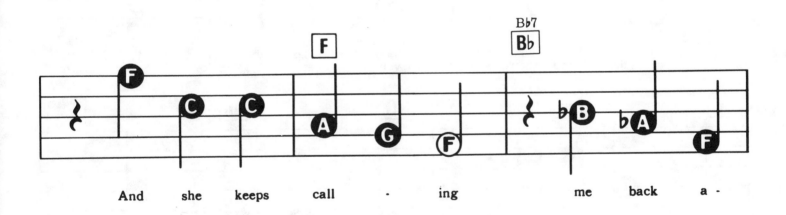

Fall - ing.    Yes,   I   am   fall - ing,

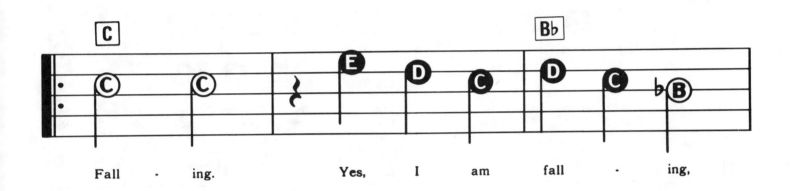

And   she   keeps   call - ing   me   back   a -

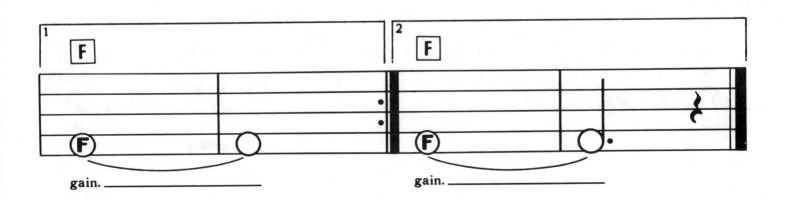

gain.                   gain.

# If

Registration 2
Rhythm: Slow Rock or Ballad

Words and Music by
David Gates

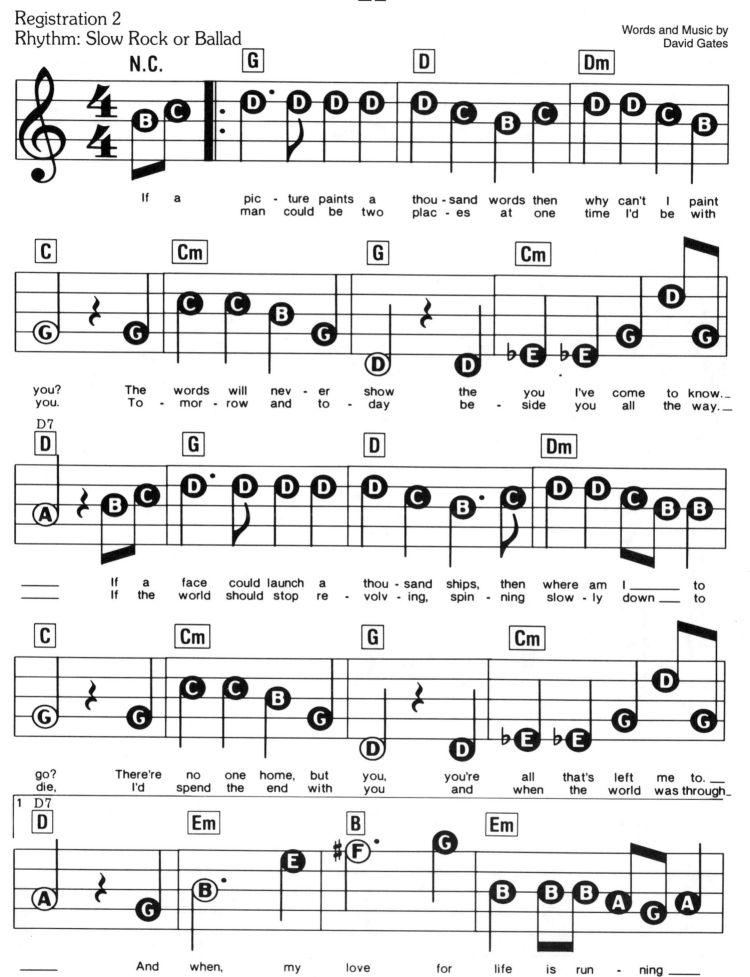

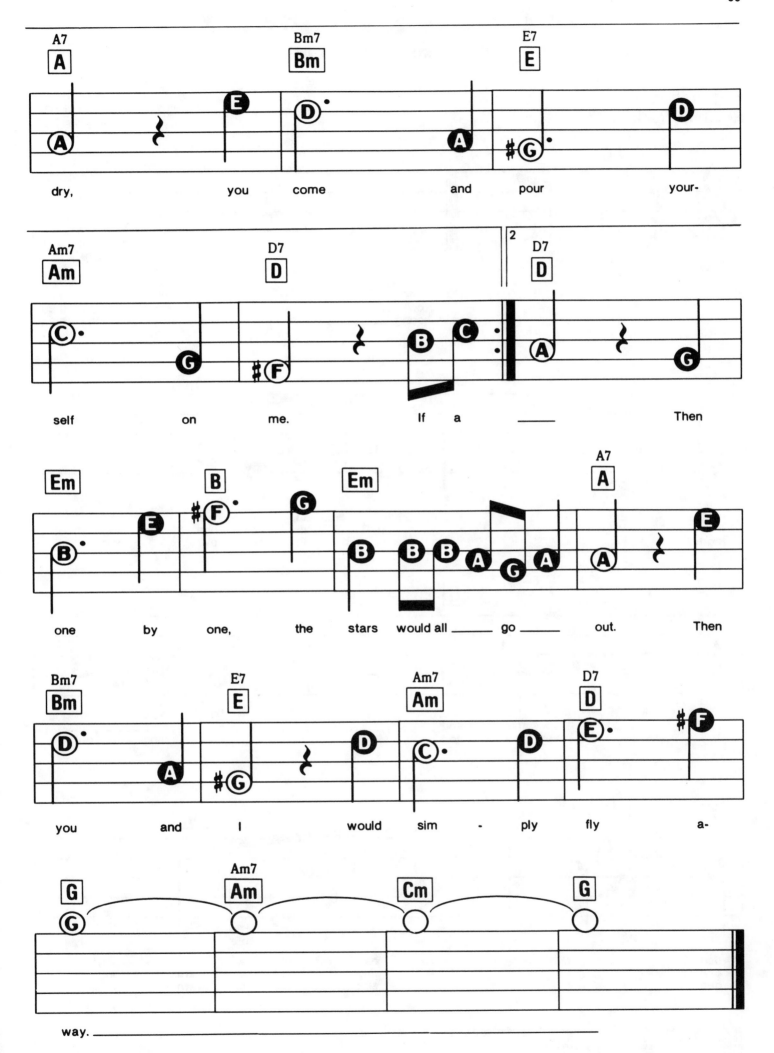

# If I Had a Hammer
## (The Hammer Song)

Registration 5
Rhythm: Rock or Slow Rock

Words and Music by Lee Hays
and Pete Seeger

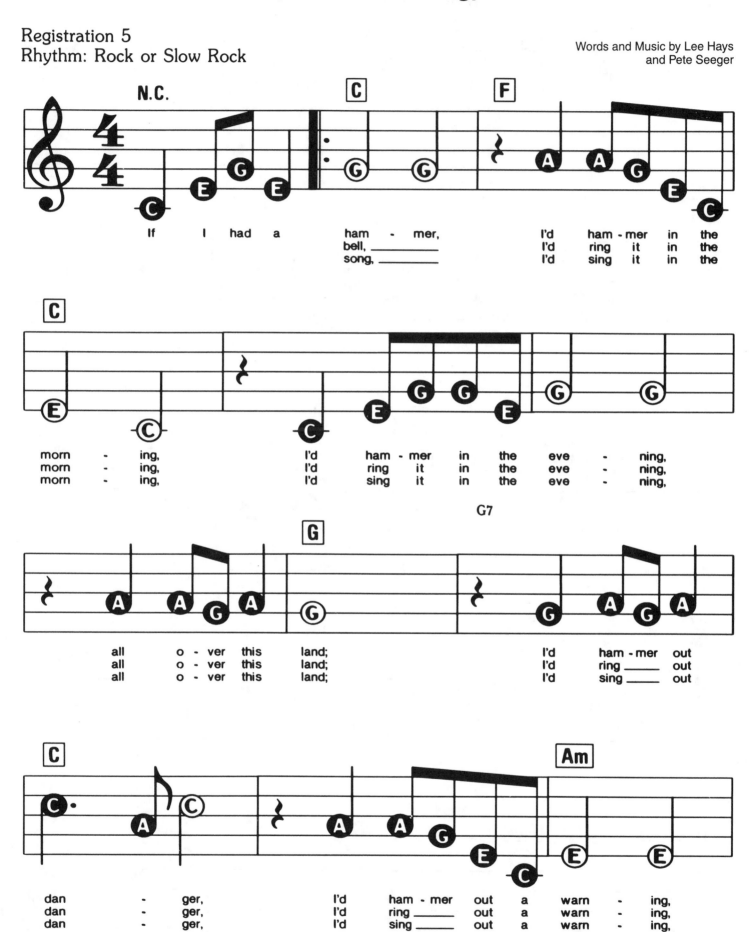

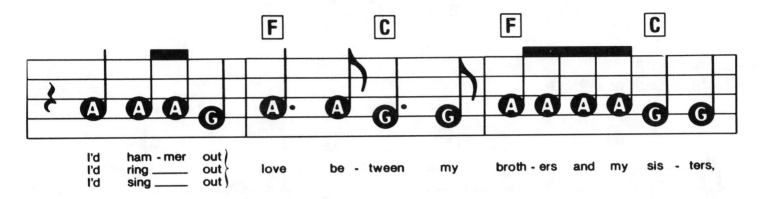

I'd ham-mer out⎱
I'd ring ____ out⎰  love be - tween my broth-ers and my sis - ters,
I'd sing ____ out⎰

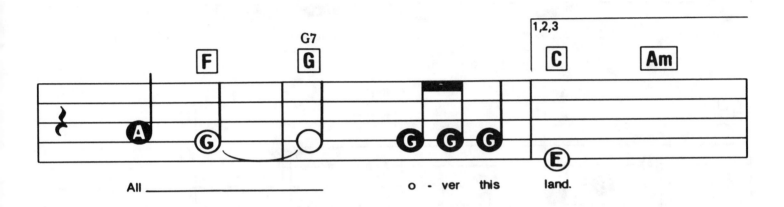

All _____  o - ver this land.

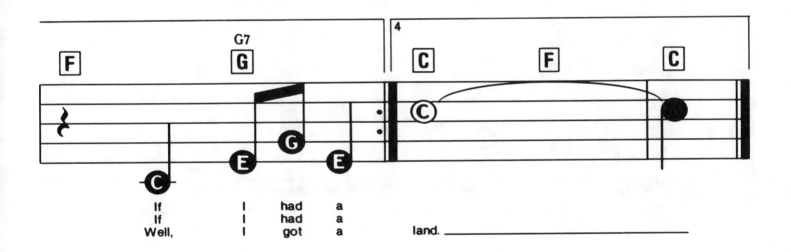

If I had a
If I had a
Well, I got a  land. _____

Additional Verse

Well, I got a hammer,
And I've got a bell,
And I've got a song to sing,
All over this land;
It's the hammer of justice,
It's the bell of freedom,
It's the song about love between my brothers and my sisters,
All over this land.

# Longer

**Registration 4**
**Rhythm: Rock or 8 Beat**

Words and Music by
Dan Fogelberg

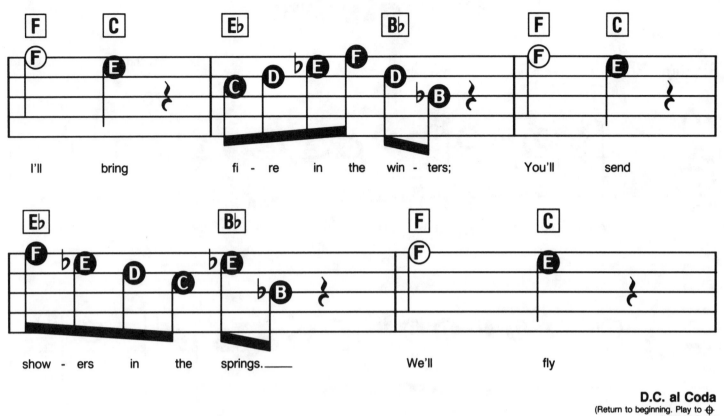

I'll    bring    fi - re    in    the    win - ters;    You'll    send

show - ers    in    the    springs.____    We'll    fly

**D.C. al Coda**
(Return to beginning. Play to ⊕
and skip to Coda)

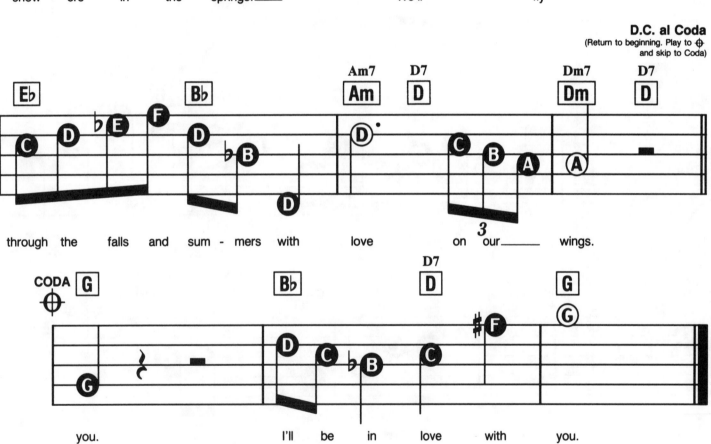

through    the    falls    and    sum - mers    with    love    on    our____    wings.

you.    I'll    be    in    love    with    you.

**Additional Lyrics**

**3.** Through the years as the fire starts to mellow,
Burning lines in the book of our lives.
Though the binding cracks and the pages start to yellow,
I'll be in love with you.

# Maggie May

Registration 9
Rhythm: Rock

Words and Music by Rod Stewart<br>and Martin Quittenton

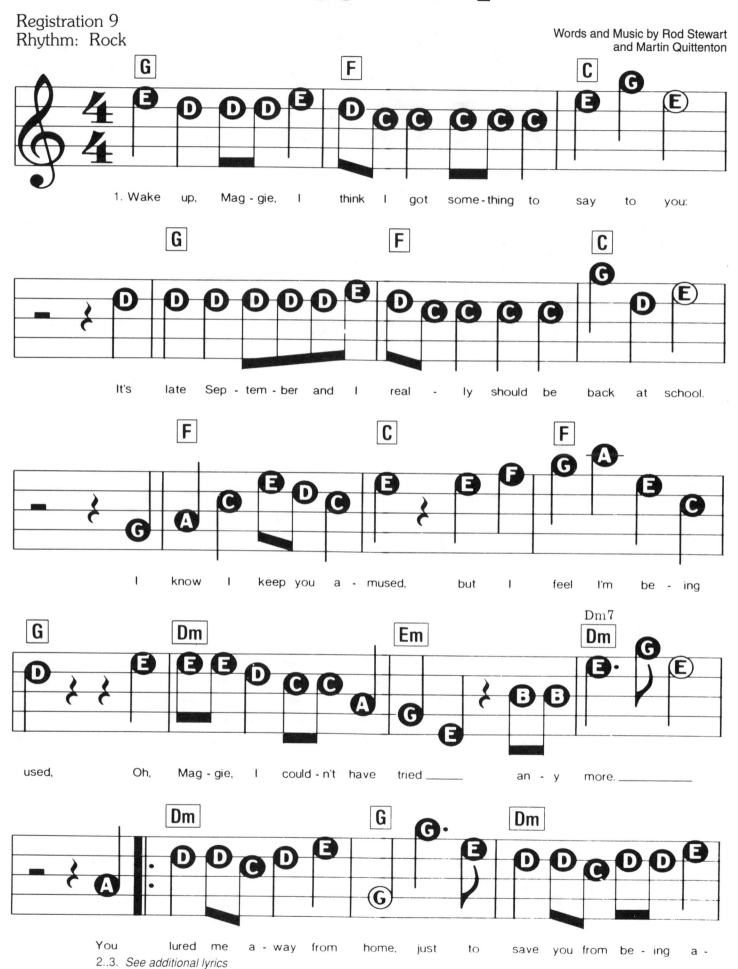

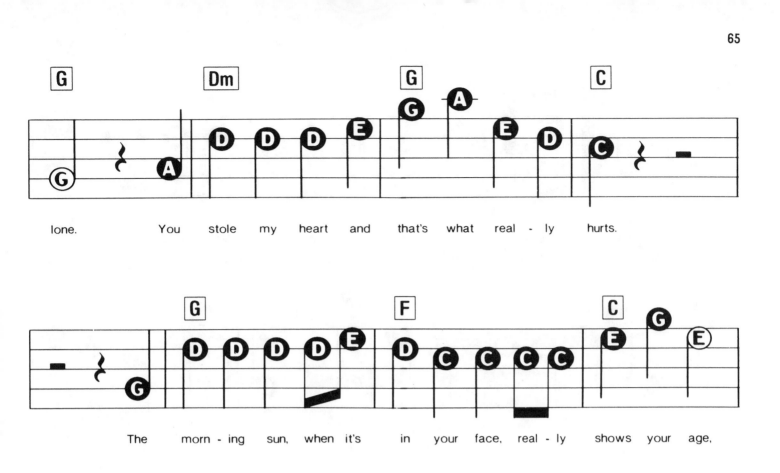

lone.　　You　stole　my　heart　and　that's　what　real - ly　hurts.

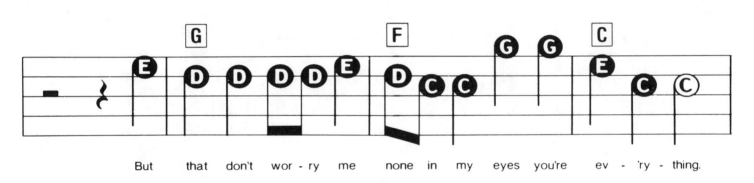

The　morn - ing　sun,　when　it's　in　your　face,　real - ly　shows　your　age,

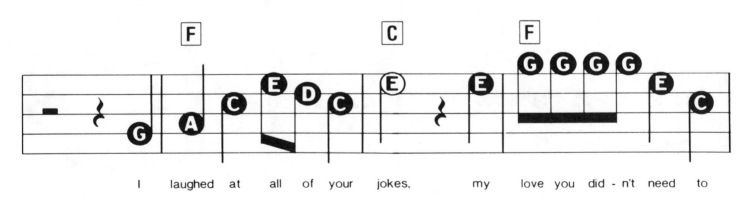

But　that　don't　wor - ry　me　none　in　my　eyes　you're　ev - 'ry - thing.

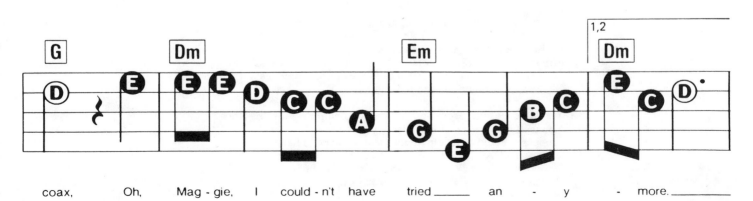

I　laughed　at　all　of　your　jokes,　my　love　you　did - n't　need　to

coax,　Oh,　Mag - gie,　I　could - n't　have　tried＿＿＿　an - y - more.＿＿＿

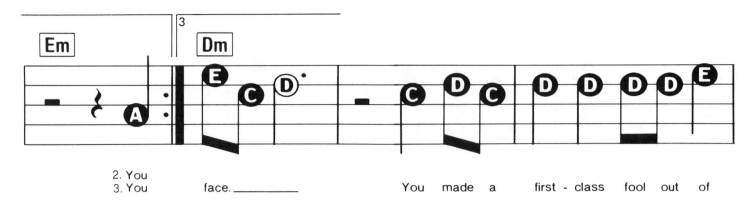

2. You
3. You face._____ You made a first - class fool out of

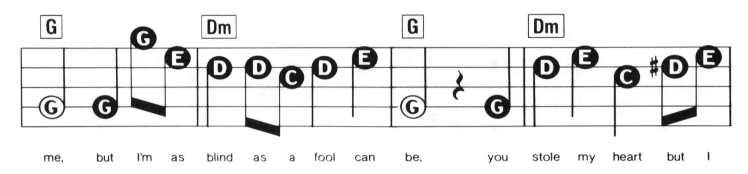

me, but I'm as blind as a fool can be, you stole my heart but I

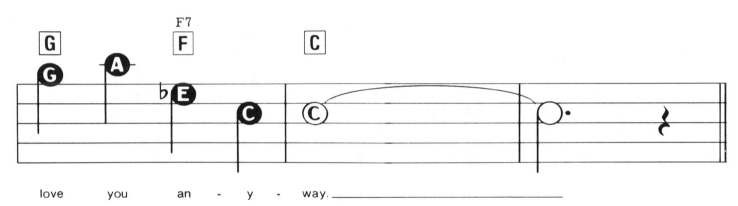

love you an - y - way._____

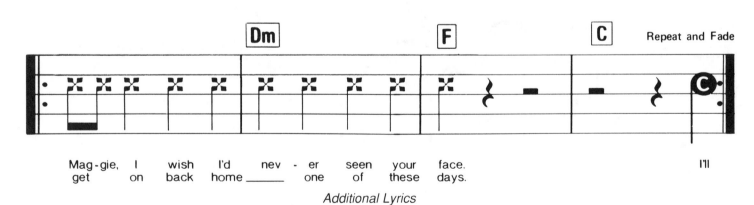

Mag - gie, I wish I'd nev - er seen your face.
get on back home_____ one of these days. I'll

*Additional Lyrics*

2. You lured me away from home, just to save you from being alone.
You stole my soul, that's a pain I can do without.
All I needed was a friend to lend a guiding hand.
But you turned into a lover, and, Mother, what a lover! You wore me out.
All you did was wreck my bed, and in the morning kick me in the head.
Oh, Maggie, I couldn't have tried any more.

3. You lured me away from home, 'cause you didn't want to be alone.
You stole my heart, I couldn't leave you if I tried.
I suppose I could collect my books and get back to school,
Or steal my Daddy's cue and make a living out of playing pool,
Or find myself a rock and roll band that needs a helpin' hand.
Oh, Maggie, I wish I'd never seen your (face).

# My Sweet Lady

Registration 2
Rhythm: Fox Trot or Ballad

Words and Music by
John Denver

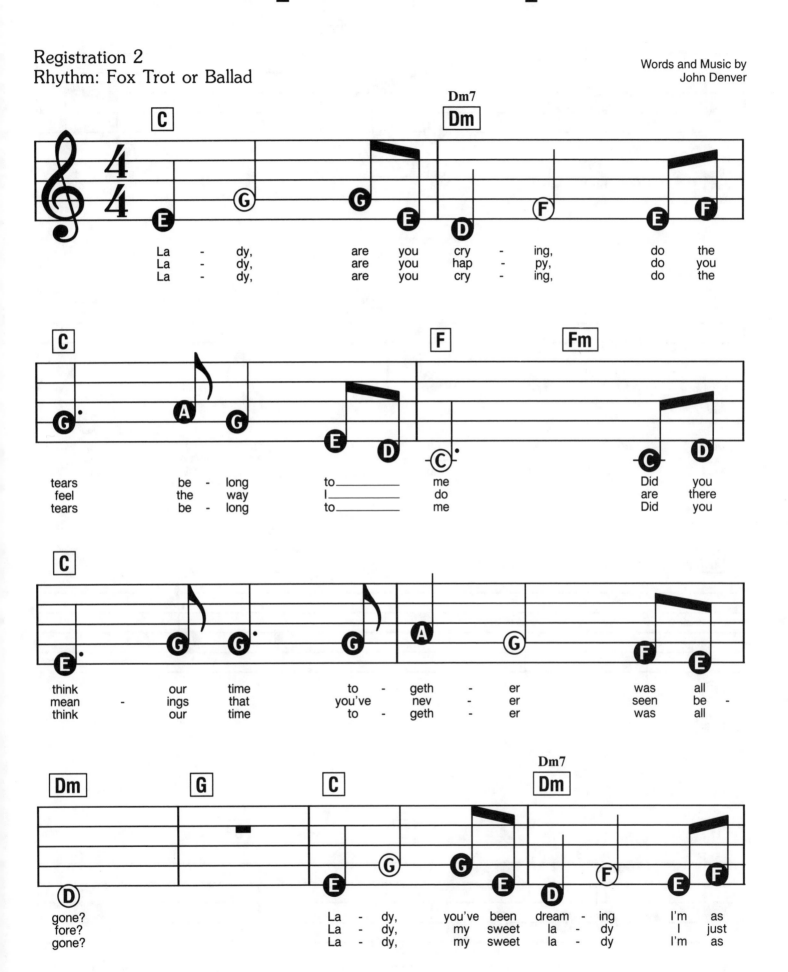

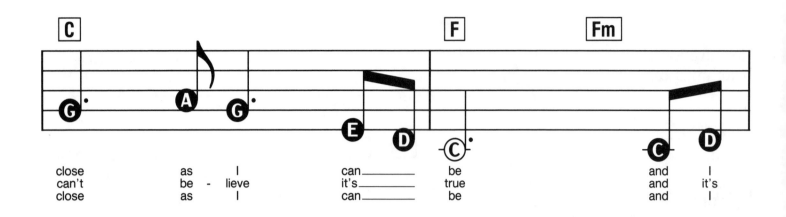

close          as          I          can_____ be                          and          I
can't          be - lieve          it's_____ true                          and          it's
close          as          I          can_____ be                          and          I

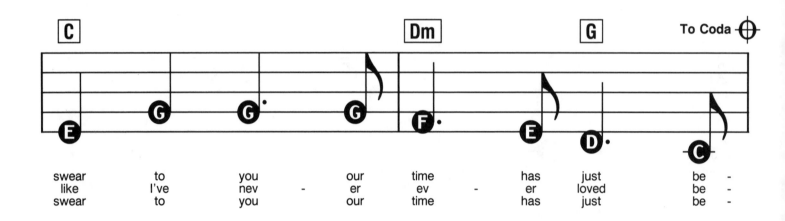

swear          to          you          our          time          has          just          be -
like          I've          nev -          er          ev -          er          loved          be -
swear          to          you          our          time          has          just          be -

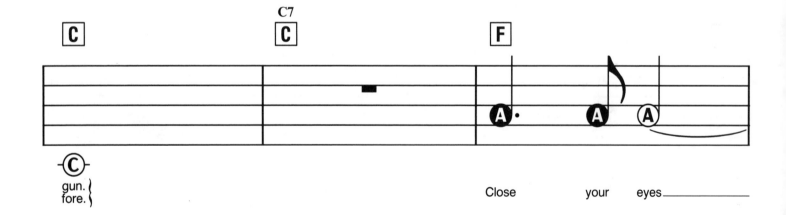

gun.
fore.          Close          your          eyes_____

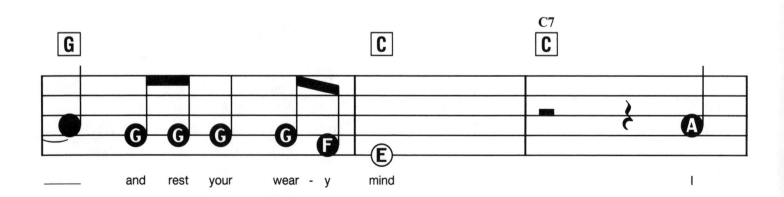

_____ and          rest          your          wear - y          mind          I

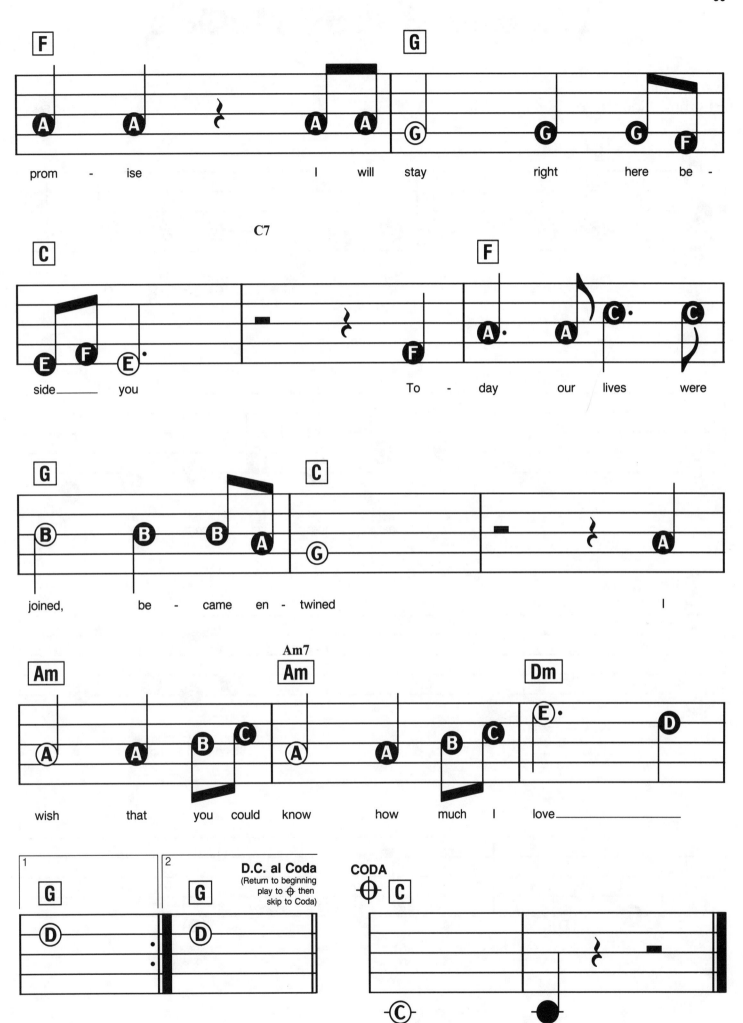

# Me and Bobby McGee

Registration 3
Rhythm: Country or Swing

Words and Music by Kris Kristofferson
and Fred Foster

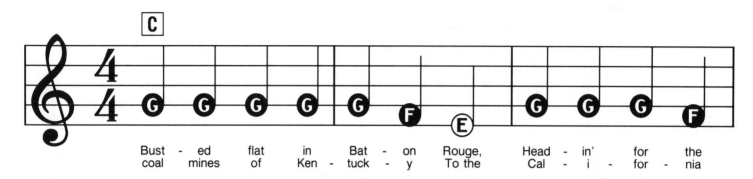

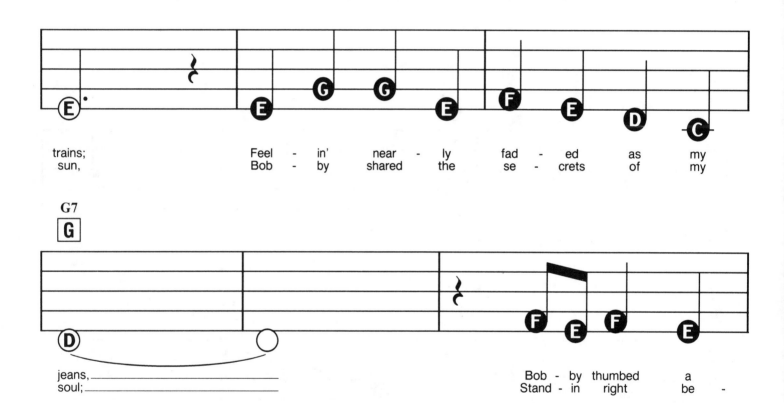

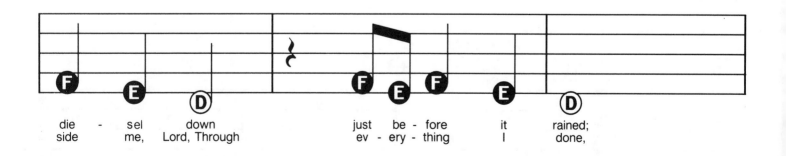

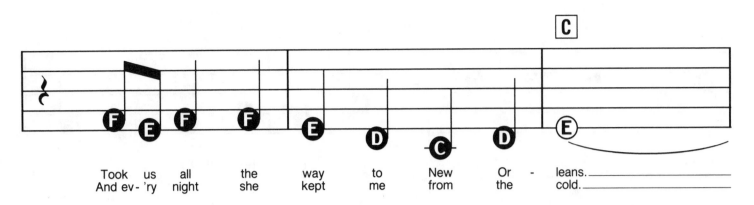

Took us all the way to New Or - leans.
And ev - 'ry night she kept me from the cold.

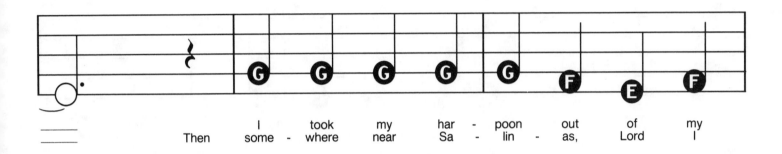

Then I took my har - poon out of my
some - where near Sa - lin - as, Lord I

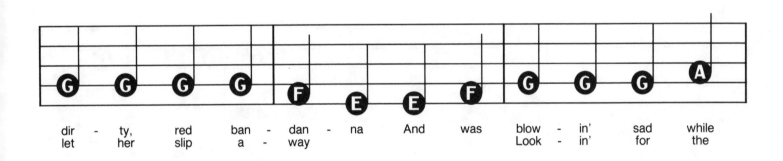

dir - ty, red ban - dan - na And was blow - in' sad while
let her slip a - way Look - in' for the

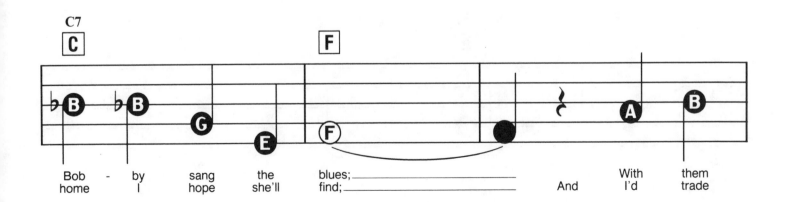

Bob - by sang the blues; And With them
home I hope she'll find; I'd trade

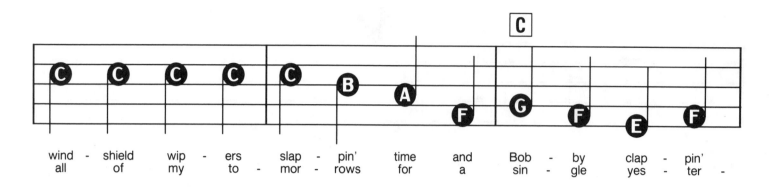

wind - shield wip - ers slap - pin' time and a Bob - by clap - pin'
all of my to - mor - rows for a sin - gle yes - ter -

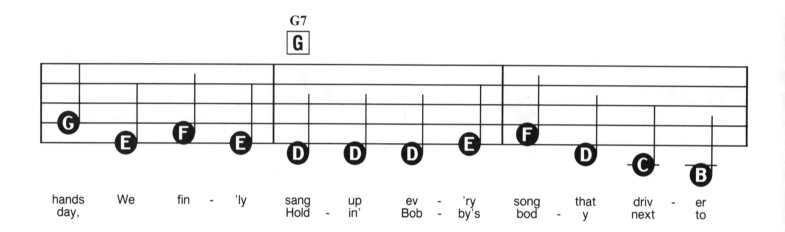

hands We fin - 'ly sang up ev - 'ry song that driv - er
day, Hold - in' Bob - by's bod - y next to

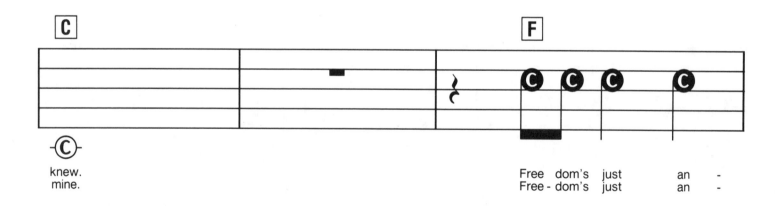

knew.
mine.

Free - dom's just an -
Free - dom's just an -

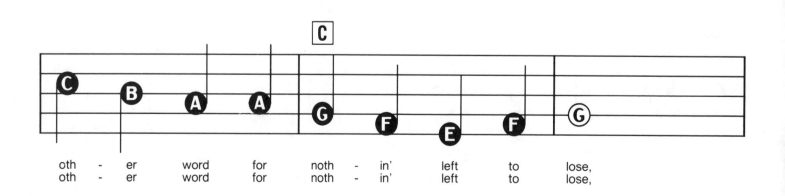

oth - er word for noth - in' left to lose,
oth - er word for noth - in' left to lose,

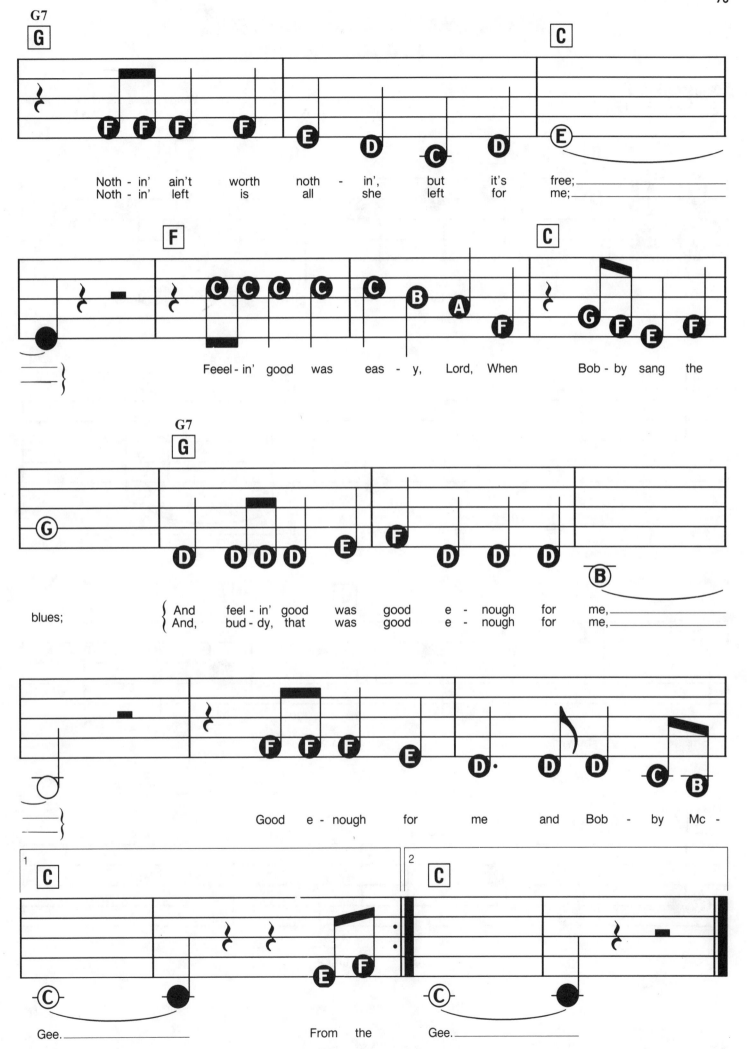

# Norwegian Wood
## (This Bird Has Flown)

Registration 2
Rhythm: Waltz

Words and Music by John Lennon
and Paul McCartney

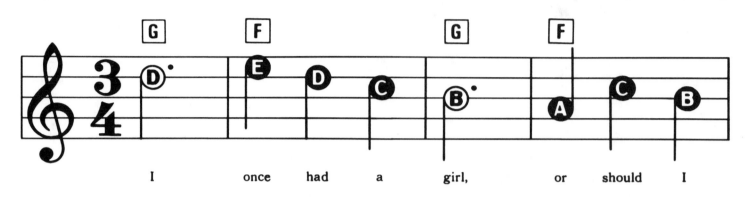

I once had a girl, or should I

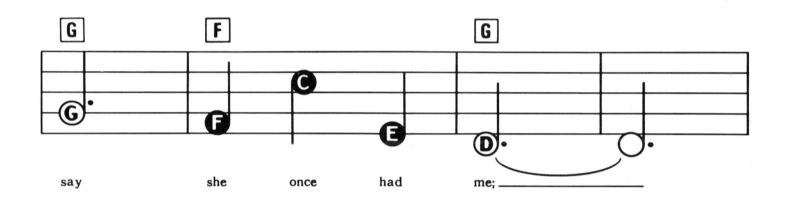

say she once had me; ____

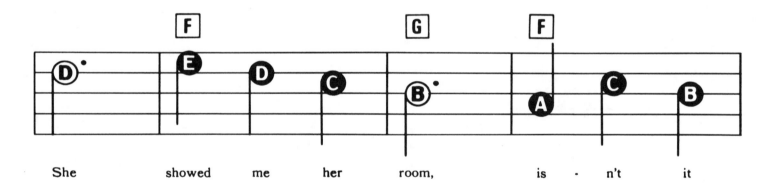

She showed me her room, is - n't it

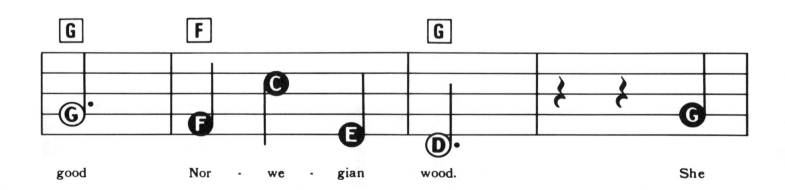

good Nor - we - gian wood. She

76

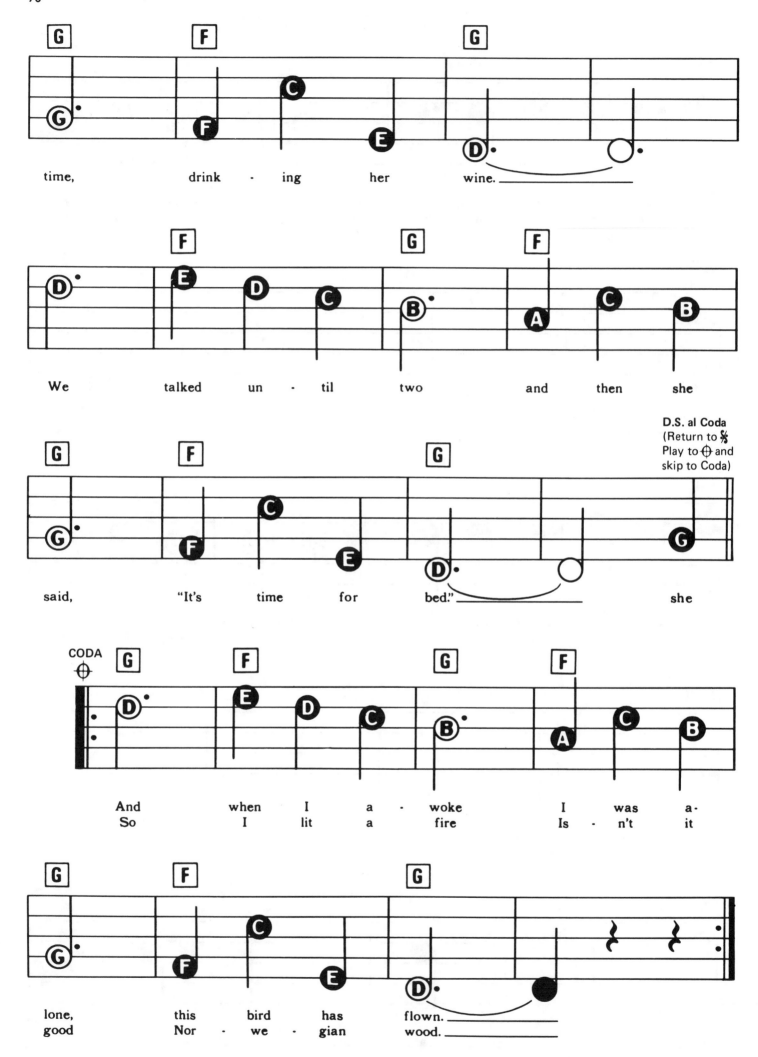

# Rocky Mountain High

Registration 4
Rhythm: Country

Words by John Denver
Music by John Denver and Mike Taylor

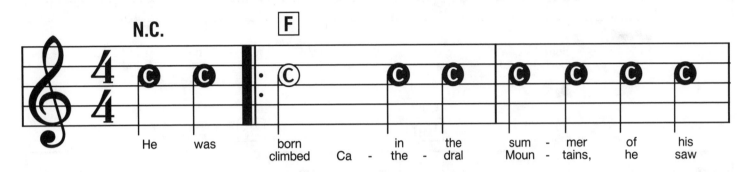

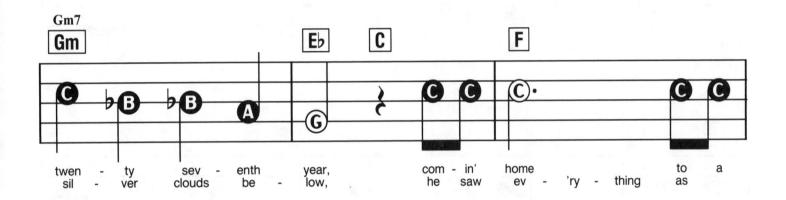

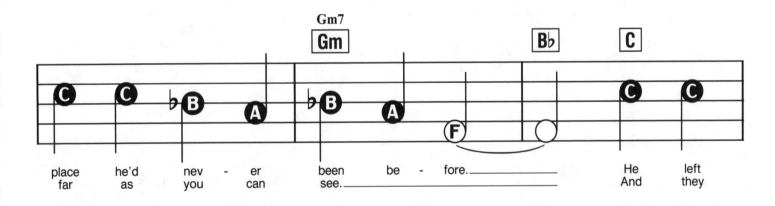

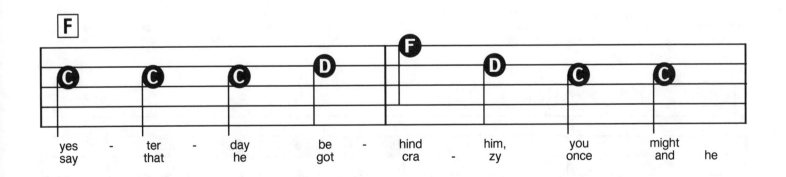

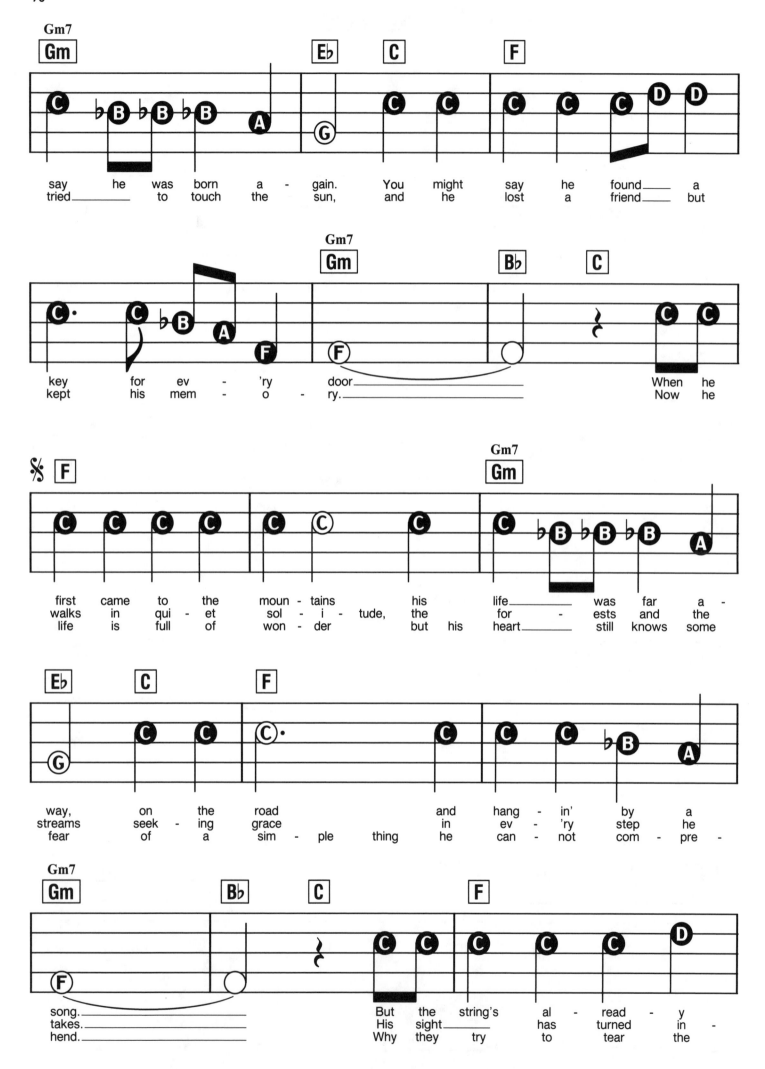

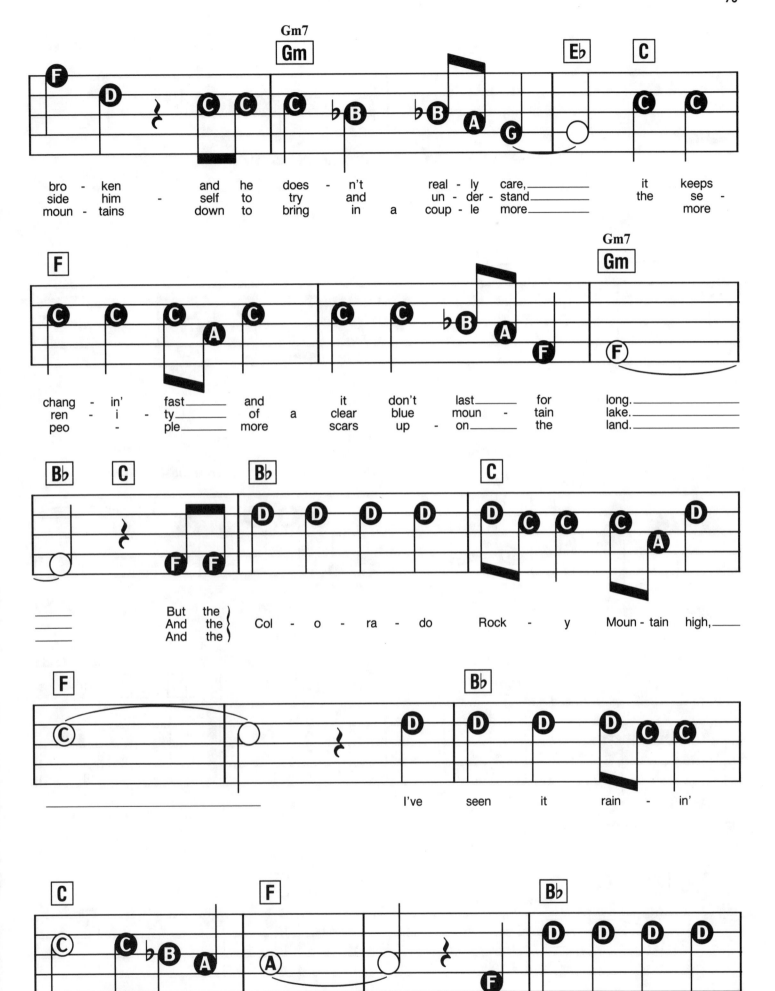

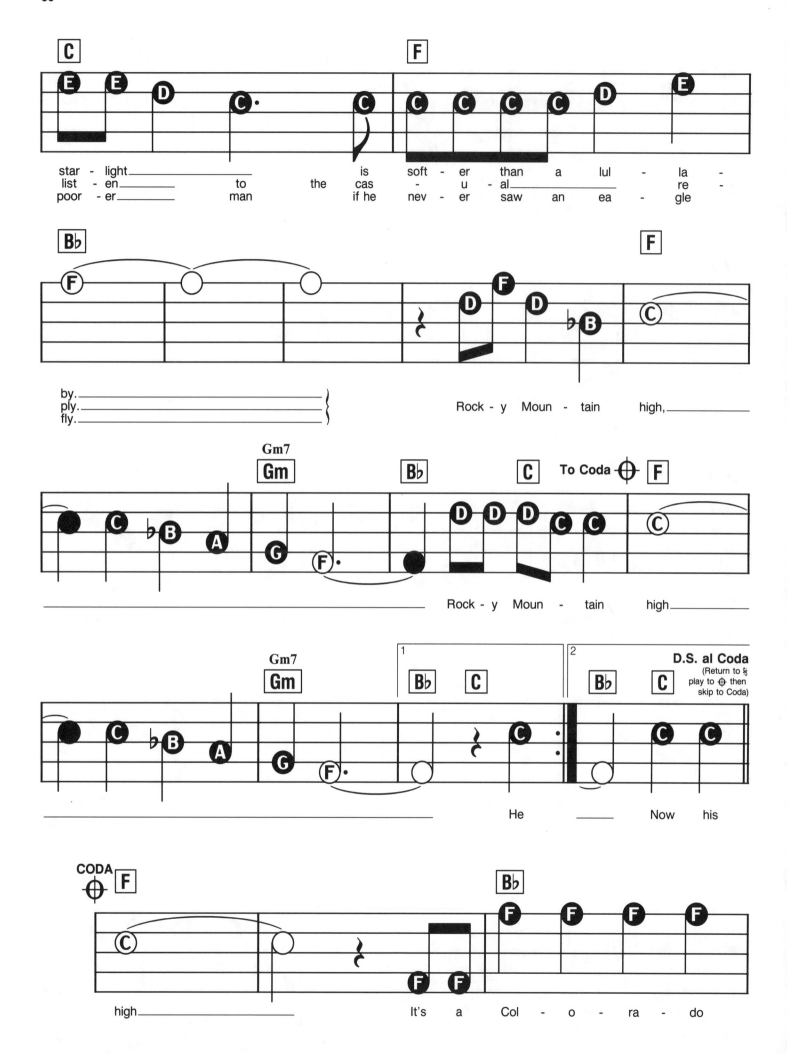

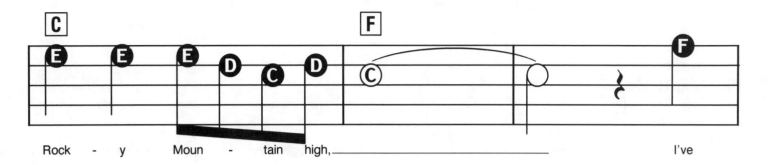

Rock - y Moun - tain high,_____ I've

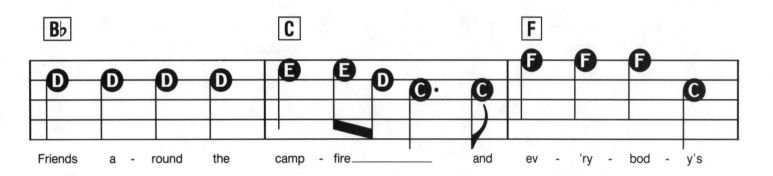

seen it rain - in' fire_____ in_____ the sky._____

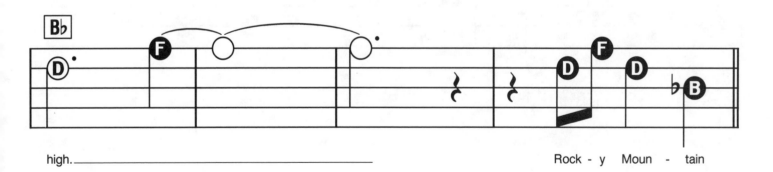

Friends a - round the camp - fire_____ and ev - 'ry - bod - y's

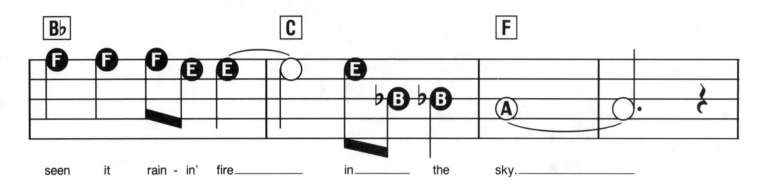

high._____ Rock - y Moun - tain

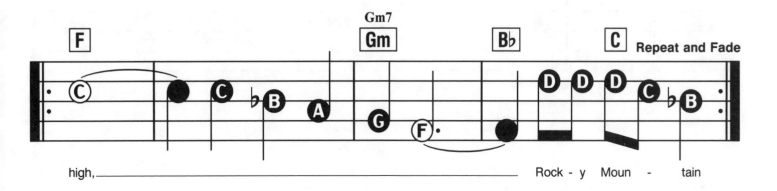

high,_____ Rock - y Moun - tain

# Part of the Plan

Registration 1
Rhythm: Rock

Words and Music by
Dan Fogelberg

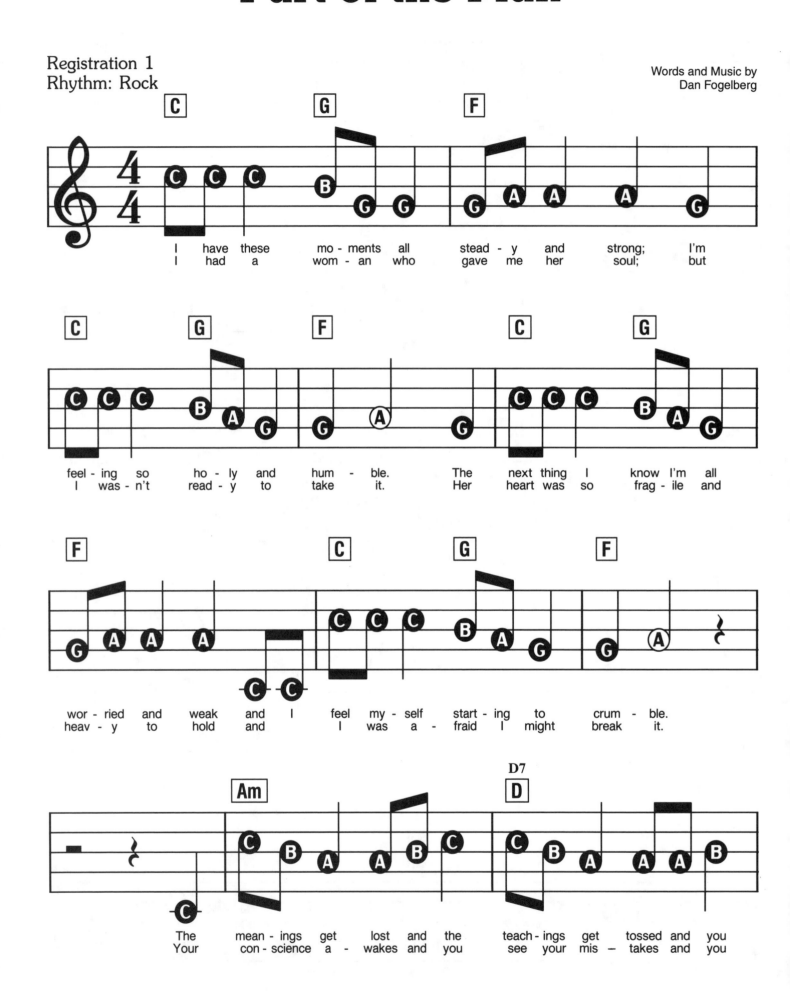

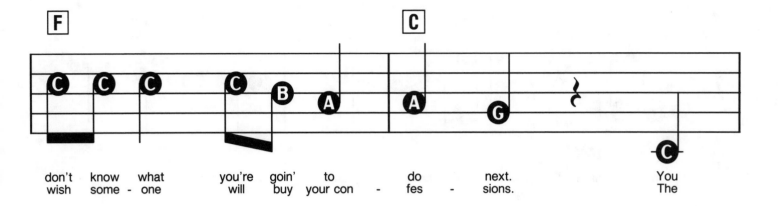

don't know what you're goin' to do next. You
wish some - one will buy your con - fes - sions. The

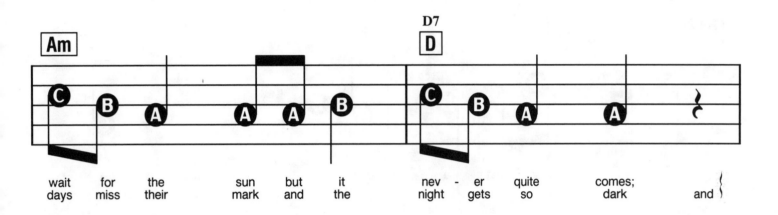

wait for the sun but it nev - er quite comes;
days miss their mark and the night gets so dark and

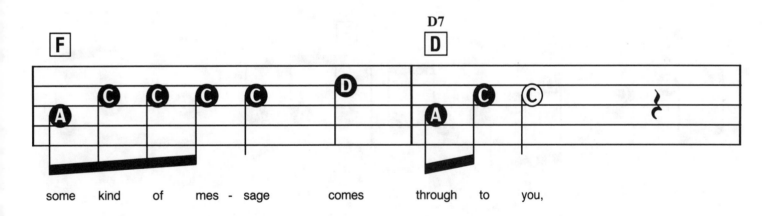

some kind of mes - sage comes through to you,

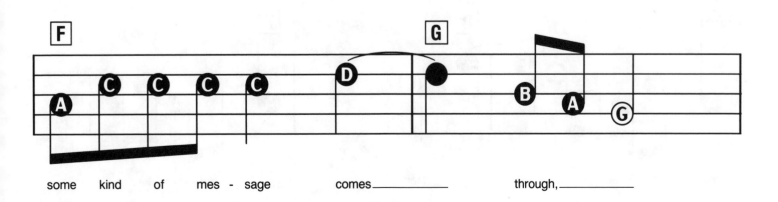

some kind of mes - sage comes_____ through,_____

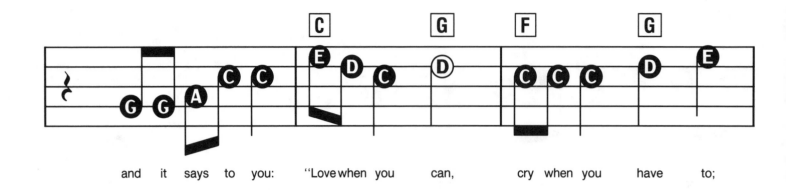

and it says to you: "Love when you can, cry when you have to;

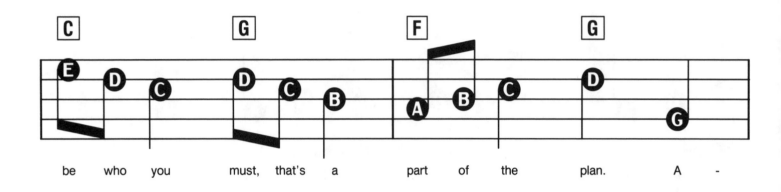

be who you must, that's a part of the plan. A -

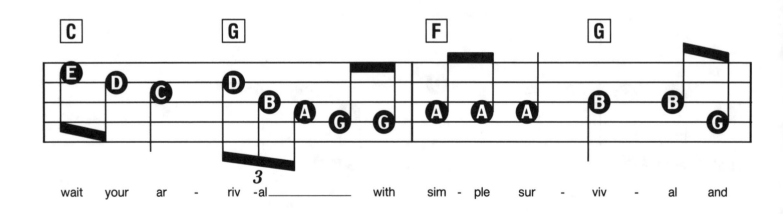

wait your ar - riv -al_____ with sim - ple sur - viv - al and

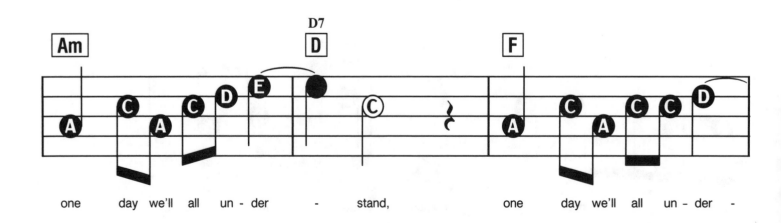

one day we'll all un - der - stand, one day we'll all un - der -

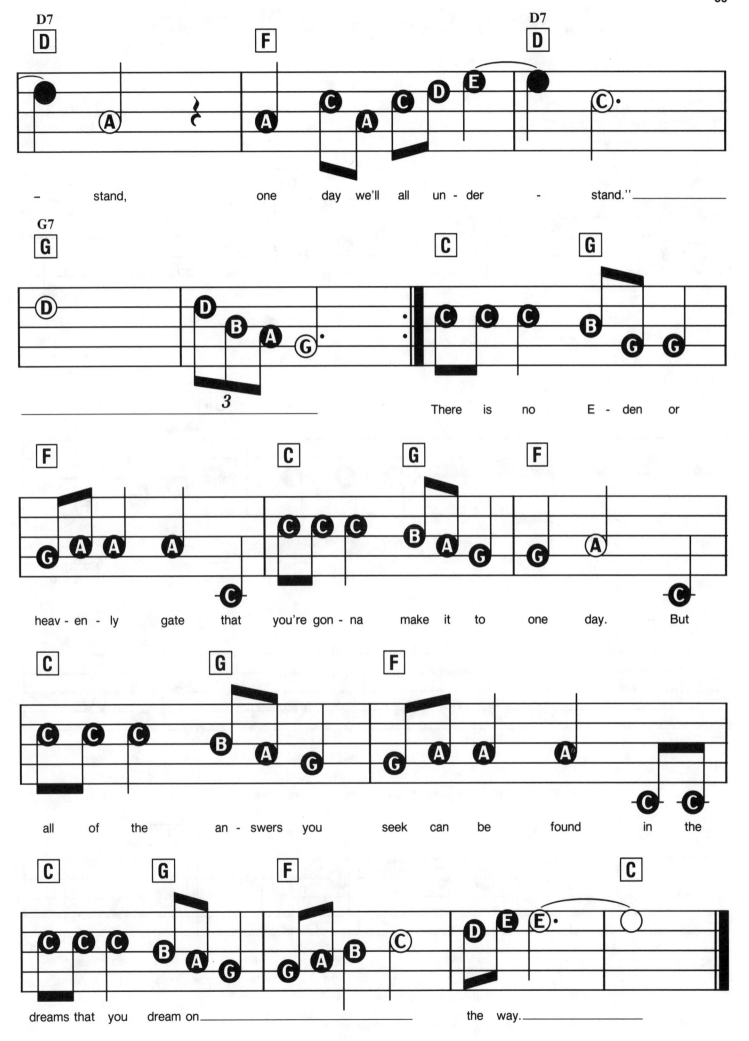

# Please Come to Boston

Registration 2
Rhythm: Rock or Ballad

Words and Music by
Dave Loggins

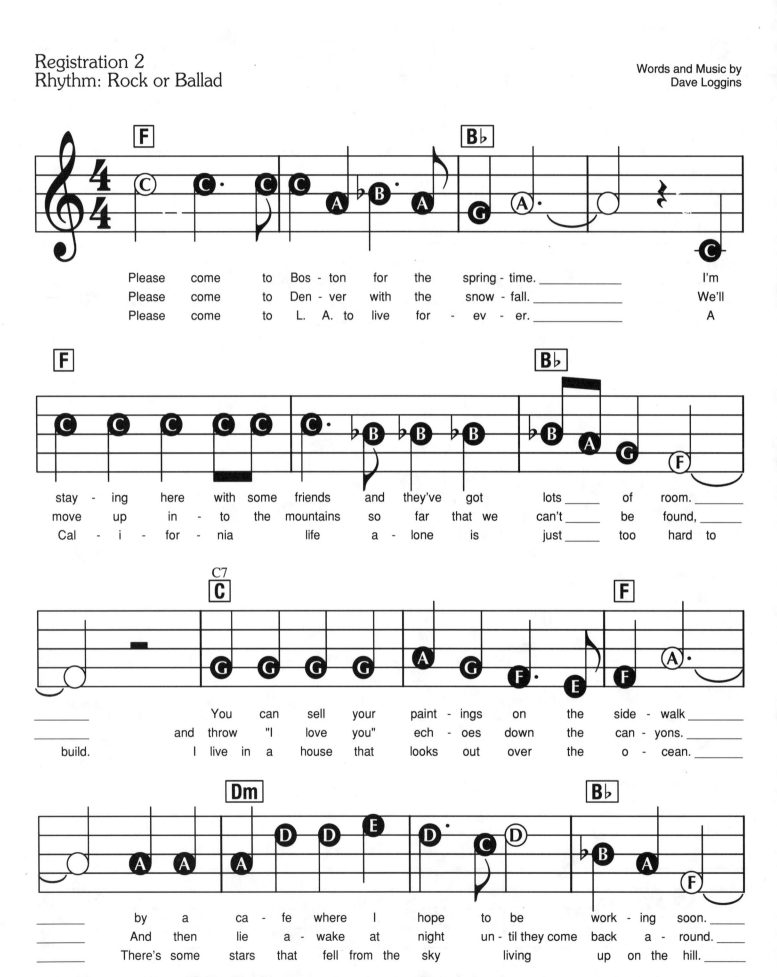

MCA music publishing

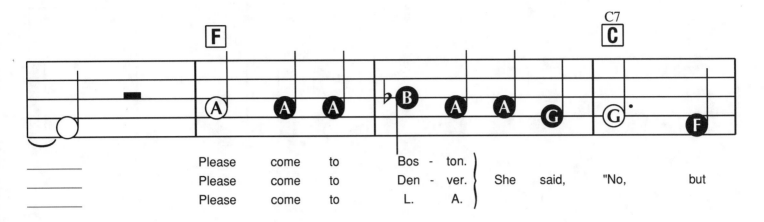

Please come to Bos - ton.
Please come to Den - ver. } She said, "No, but
Please come to L. A.

you come home to me." And she said, "Hey ram - blin' boy, now won't you

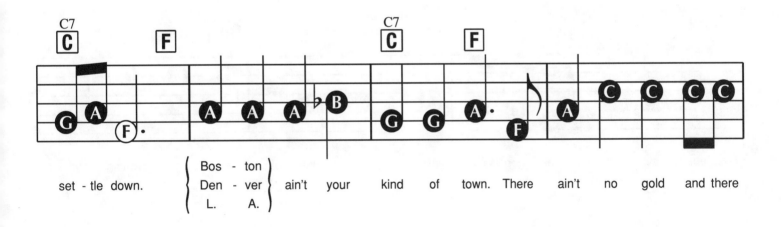

set - tle down. { Bos - ton / Den - ver / L. A. } ain't your kind of town. There ain't no gold and there

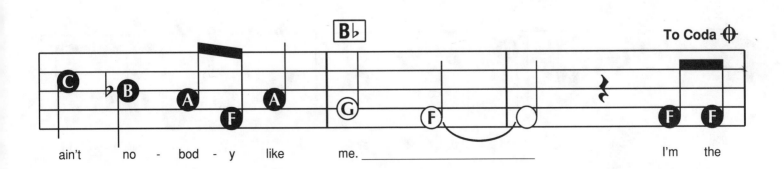

To Coda ⊕

ain't no - bod - y like me. _____ I'm the

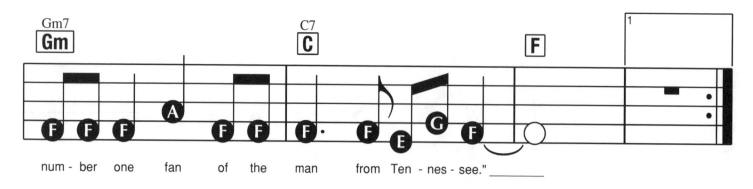

num - ber one fan of the man from Ten - nes - see." _____

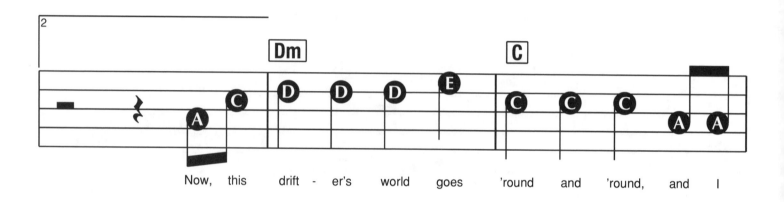

Now, this drift - er's world goes 'round and 'round, and I

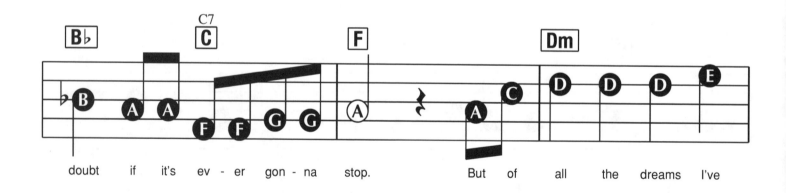

doubt if it's ev - er gon - na stop. But of all the dreams I've

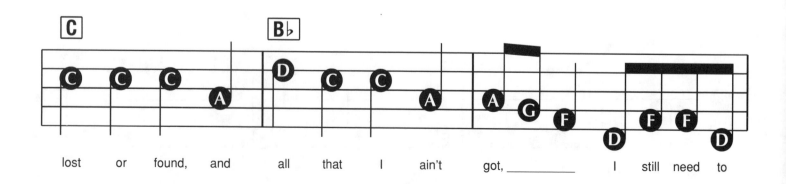

lost or found, and all that I ain't got, _____ I still need to

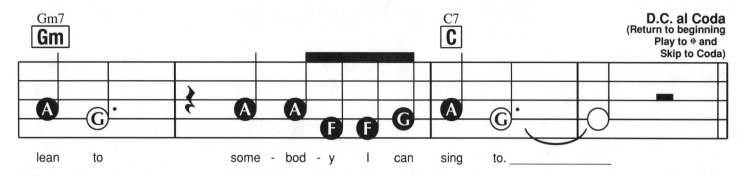

lean to    some - bod - y I can sing to. _____

**CODA**

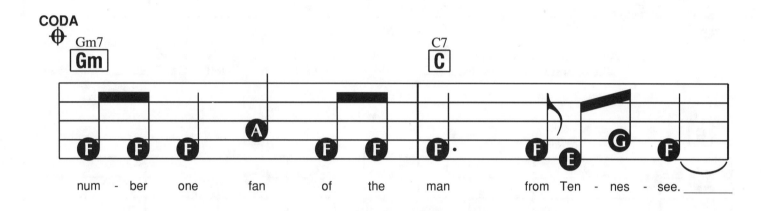

num - ber one fan of the man    from Ten - nes - see. _____

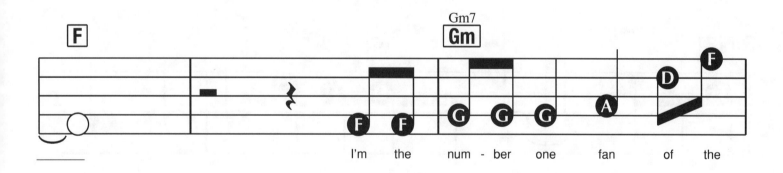

____    I'm the num - ber one fan of the

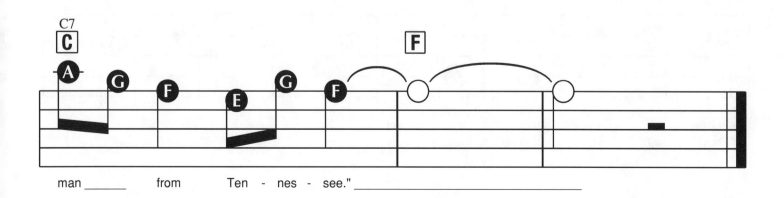

man _____ from Ten - nes - see." _____

# Rocky Raccoon

Registration 5
Rhythm: 2-beat or Swing

Words and Music by John Lennon
and Paul McCartney

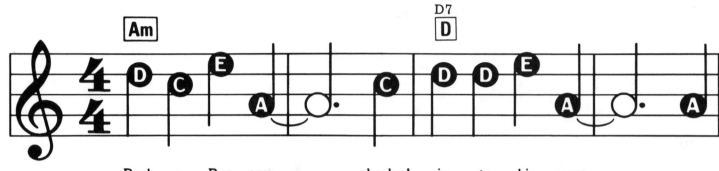

Rock - y Rac - coon _____ checked in - to his room _____
She and her man _____ who called him - self Dan _____ were

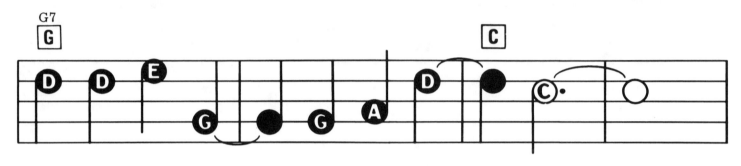

on - ly to find _____ Gid - eon's Bi - ble. _____
in the next room _____ at the hoe - down. _____

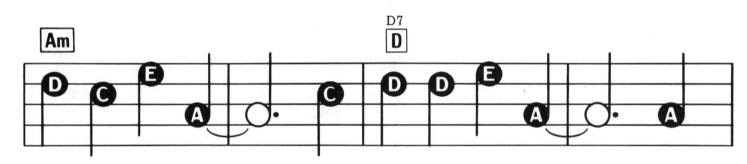

Rock - y had come _____ e - quipped with a gun _____ to
Rock - y burst in _____ and grin - ning a grin, _____ He said,

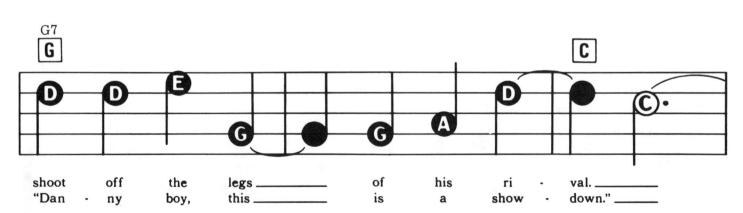

shoot off the legs _____ of his ri - val. _____
"Dan - ny boy, this _____ is a show - down." _____

# Summer Breeze

Registration 7
Rhythm: Moderate Rock Ballad

Words and Music by James Seals
and Dash Crofts

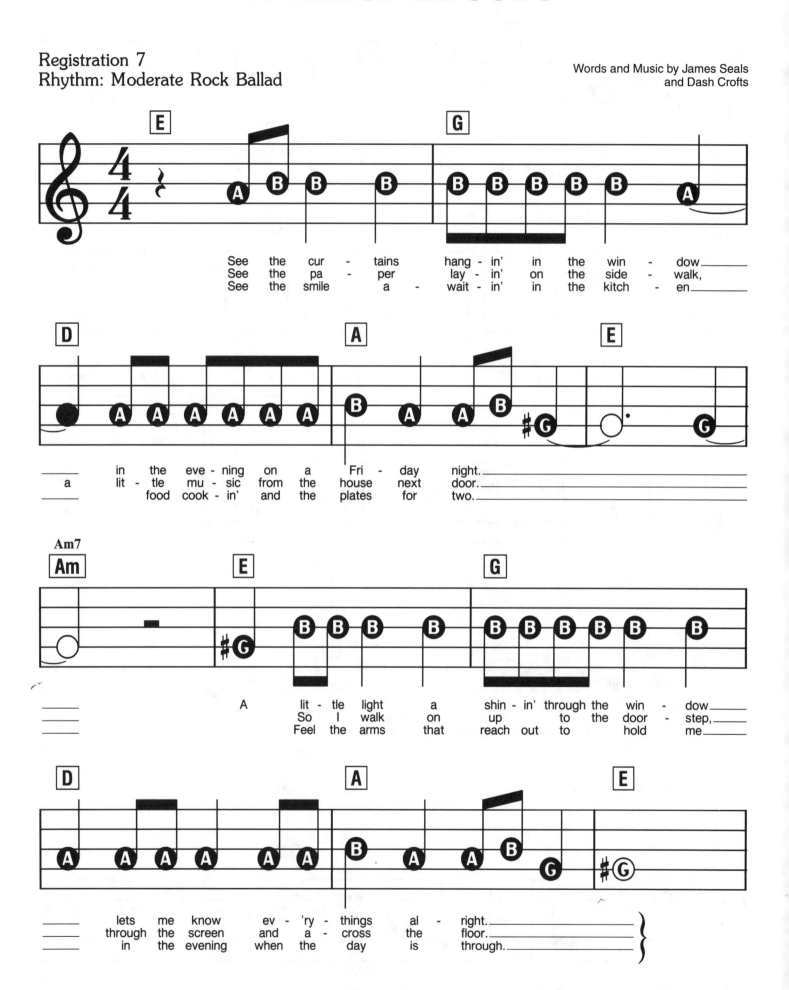

MCA music publishing

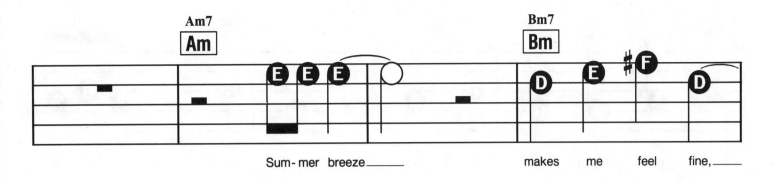

Sum-mer breeze_____ makes me feel fine,_____

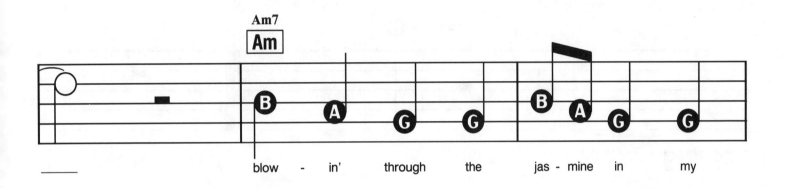

_____ blow - in' through the jas - mine in my

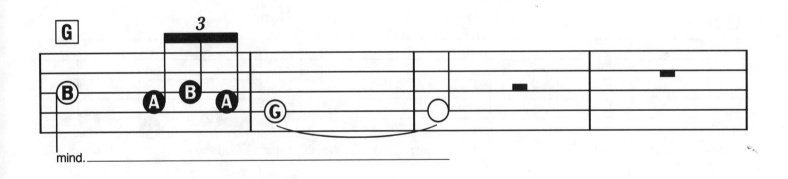

mind._____

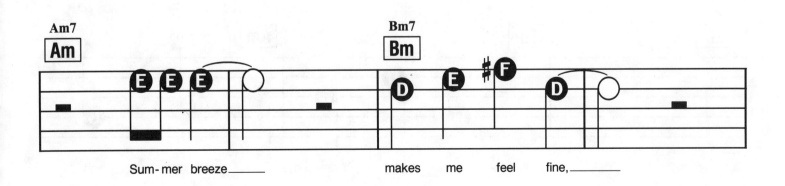

Sum-mer breeze_____ makes me feel fine,_____

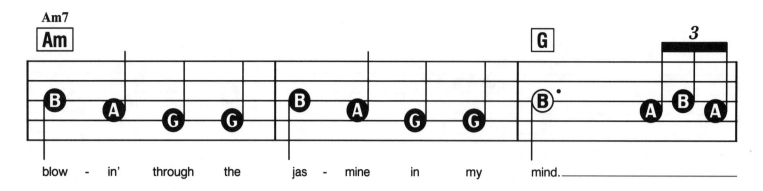

blow - in' through the jas - mine in my mind.

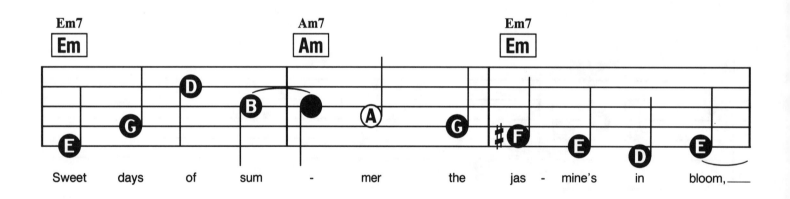

To Coda

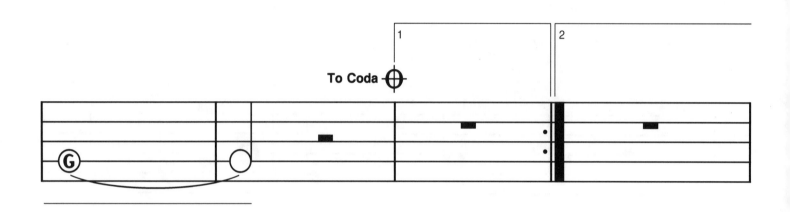

Sweet days of sum - mer the jas - mine's in bloom,

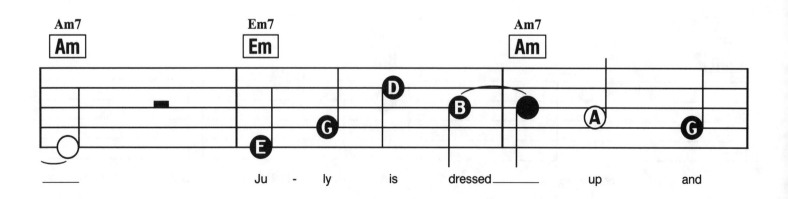

Ju - ly is dressed up and

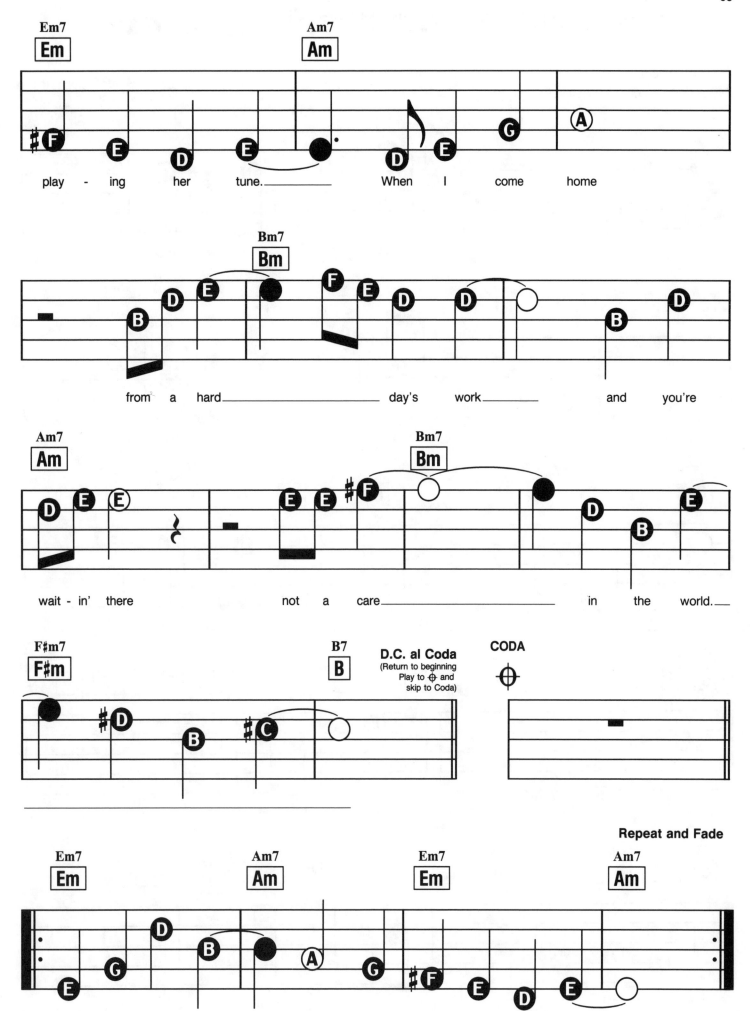

# Sunshine on My Shoulders

Registration 1
Rhythm: Fox Trot or Ballad

Words by John Denver
Music by John Denver, Mike Taylor and Dick Kniss

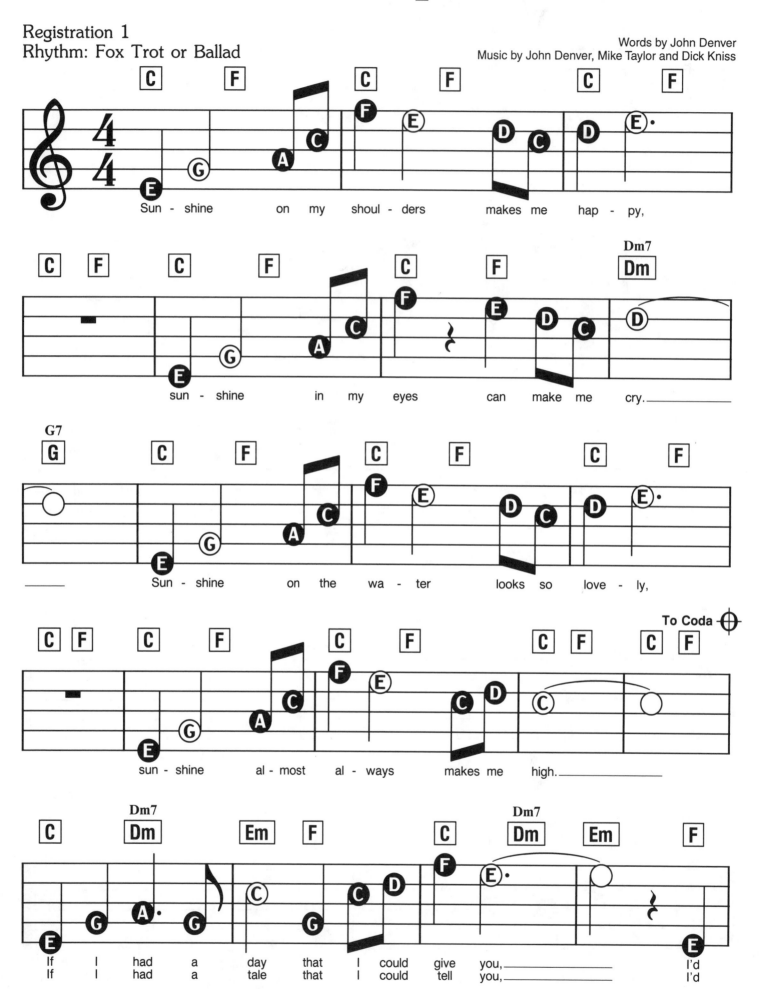

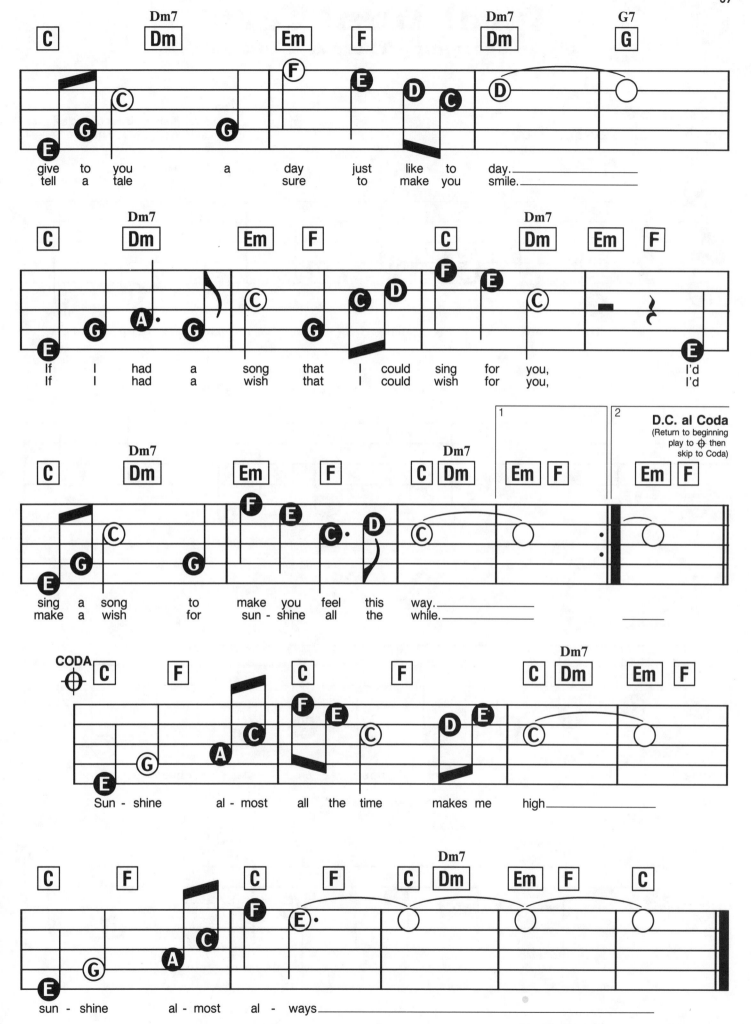

# Turn! Turn! Turn!
## (To Everything There Is a Season)

Registration 2
Rhythm: Ballad or Fox Trot

Words from the Book of Ecclesiastes
Adaptation and Music by Pete Seeger

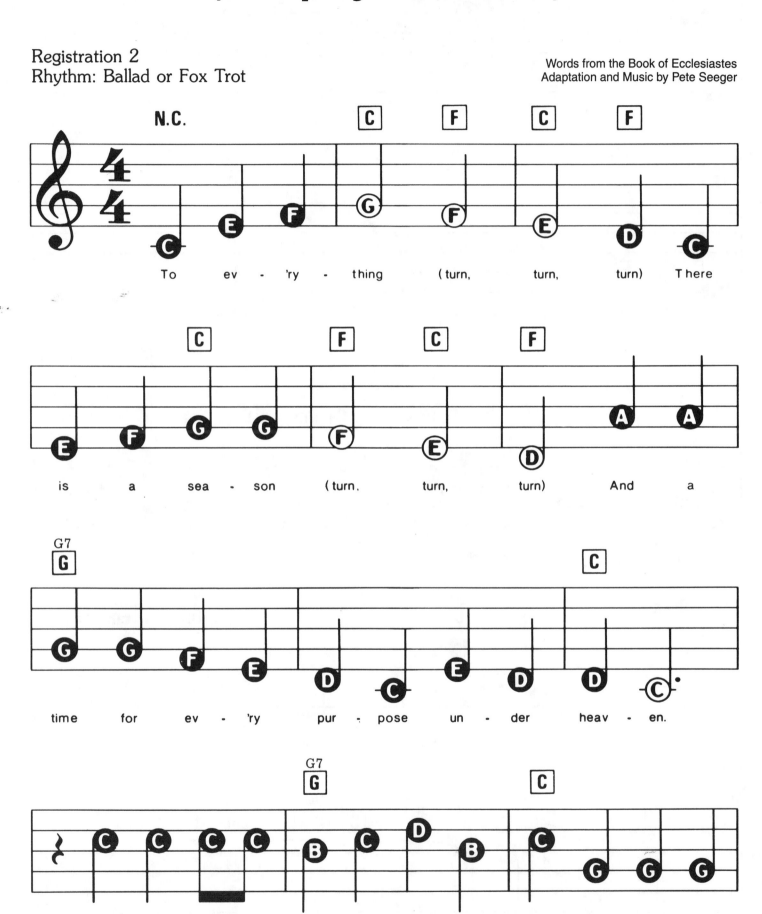

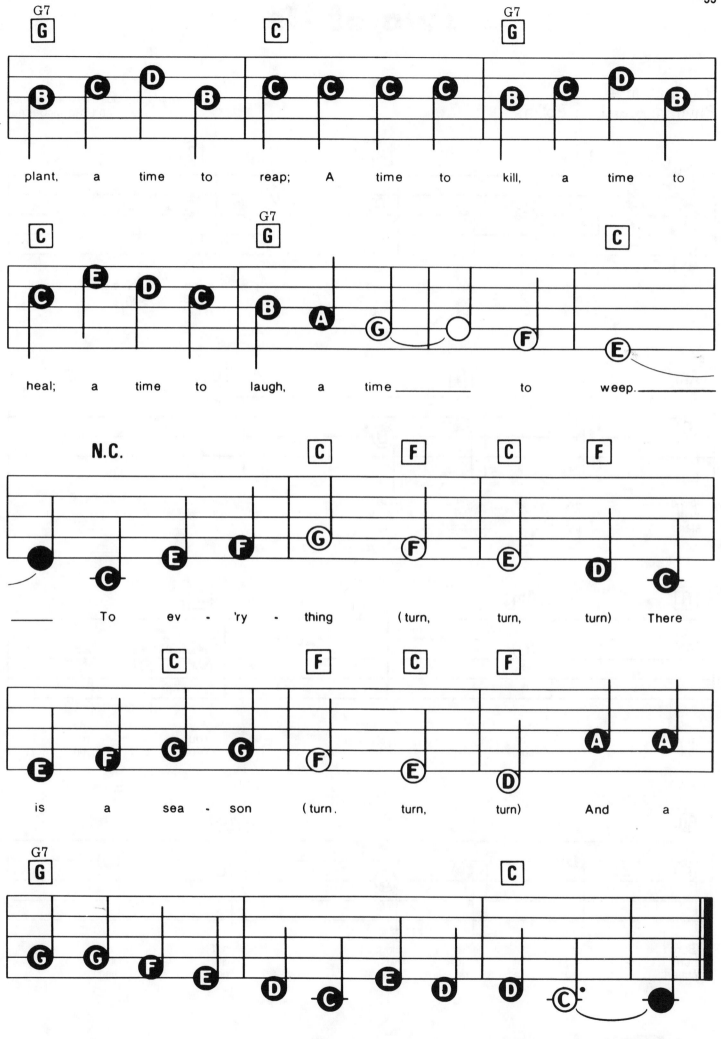

# Two of Us

Registration 4
Rhythm: March or Polka

Words and Music by John Lennon
and Paul McCartney

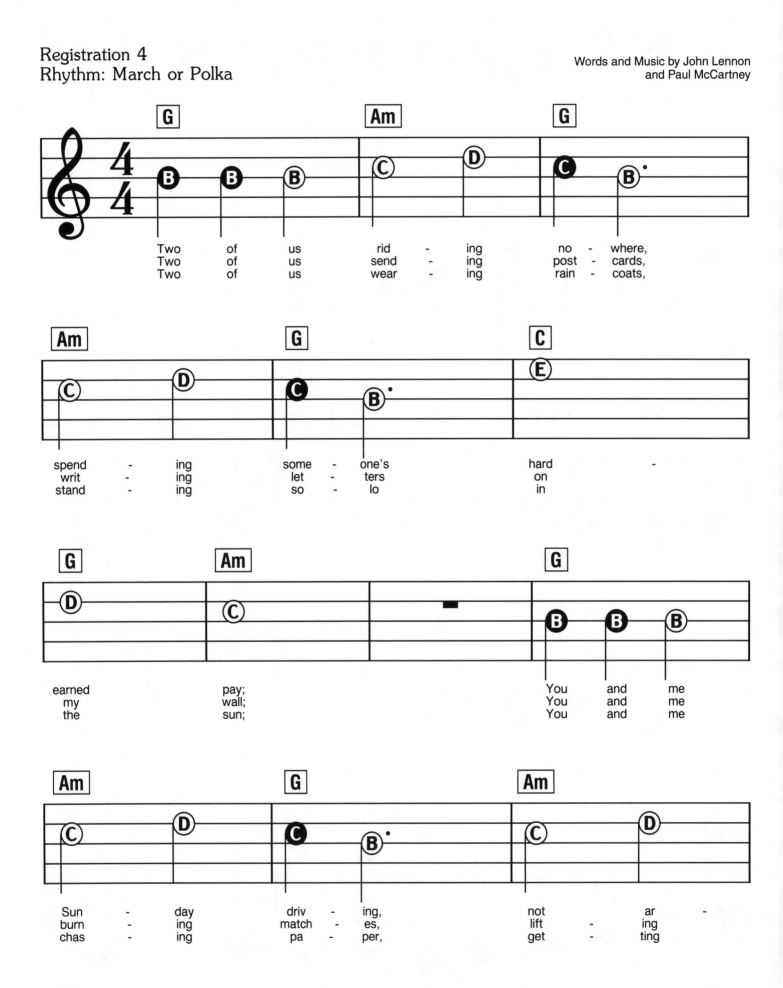

Two of us rid - ing no - where,
Two of us send - ing post - cards,
Two of us wear - ing rain - coats,

spend - ing some - one's hard -
writ - ing let - ters on
stand - ing so - lo in

earned pay;
my wall;
the sun;

You and me
You and me
You and me

Sun - day driv - ing, not ar -
burn - ing match - es, lift - ing
chas - ing pa - per, get - ting

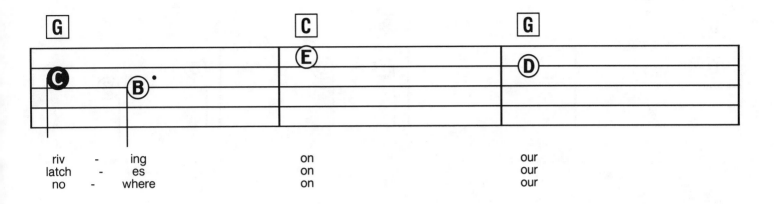

riv - ing          on          our
latch - es          on          our
no - where          on          our

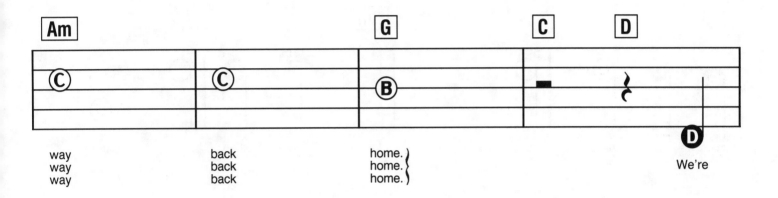

way        back        home.
way        back        home.
way        back        home.        We're

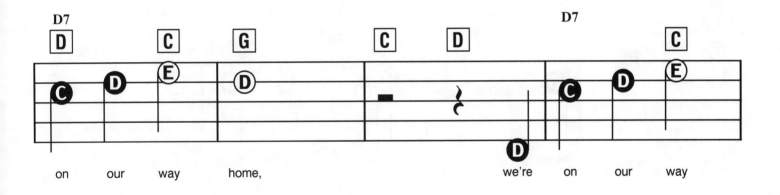

on    our    way    home,        we're    on    our    way

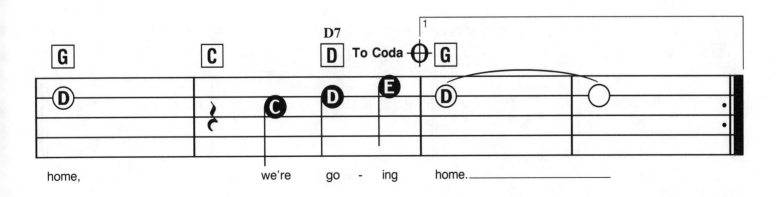

home,        we're    go - ing    home.

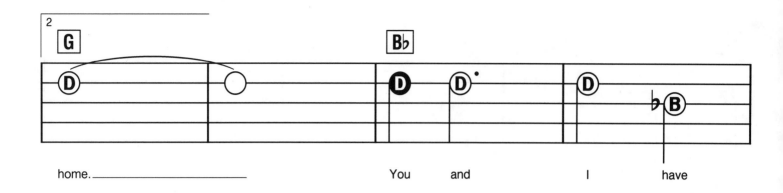

home._____ You and I have

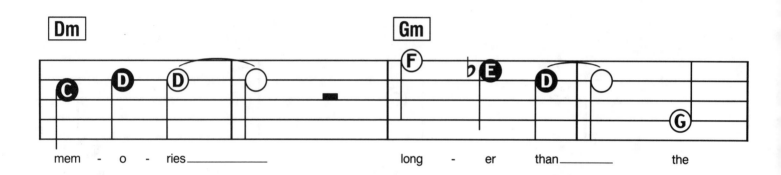

mem - o - ries_____ long - er than_____ the

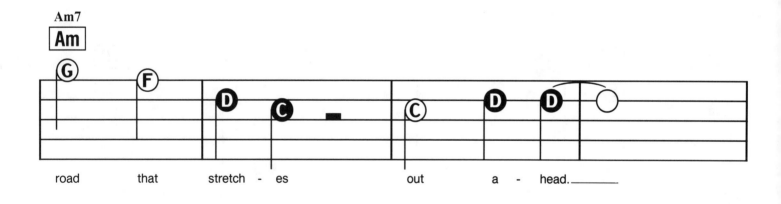

road that stretch - es out a - head._____

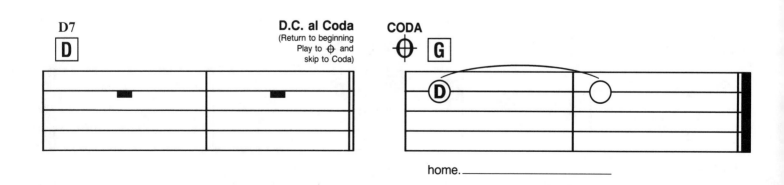

home._____

# You've Got a Friend

Registration 3
Rhythm: Slow Rock or Ballad

Words and Music by
Carole King

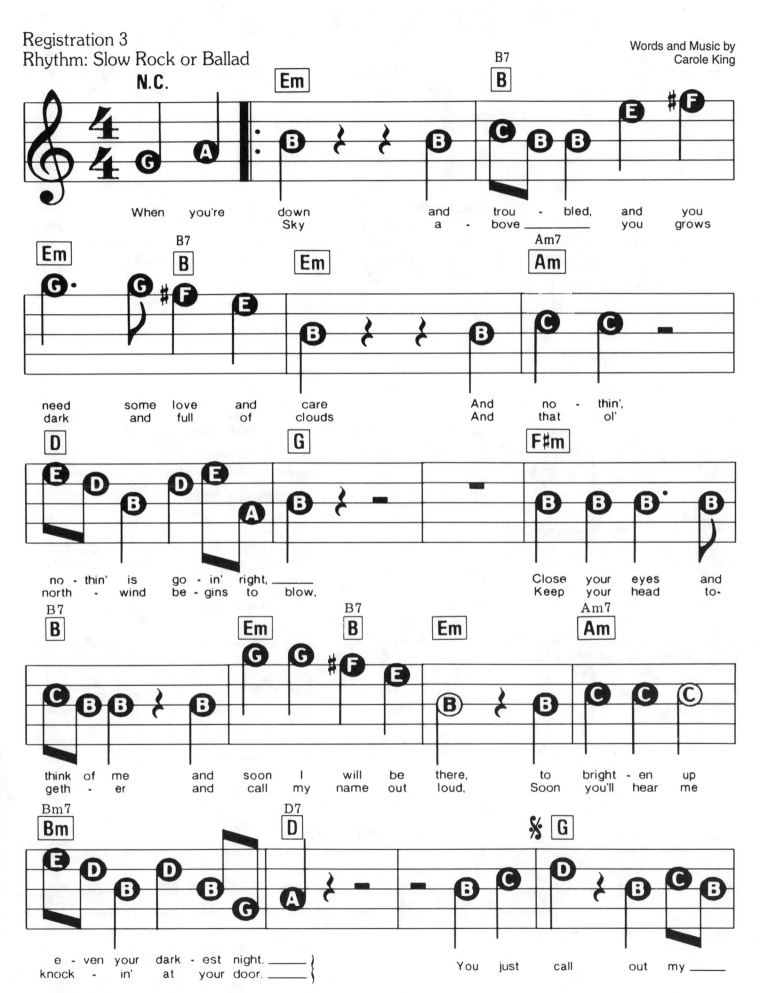

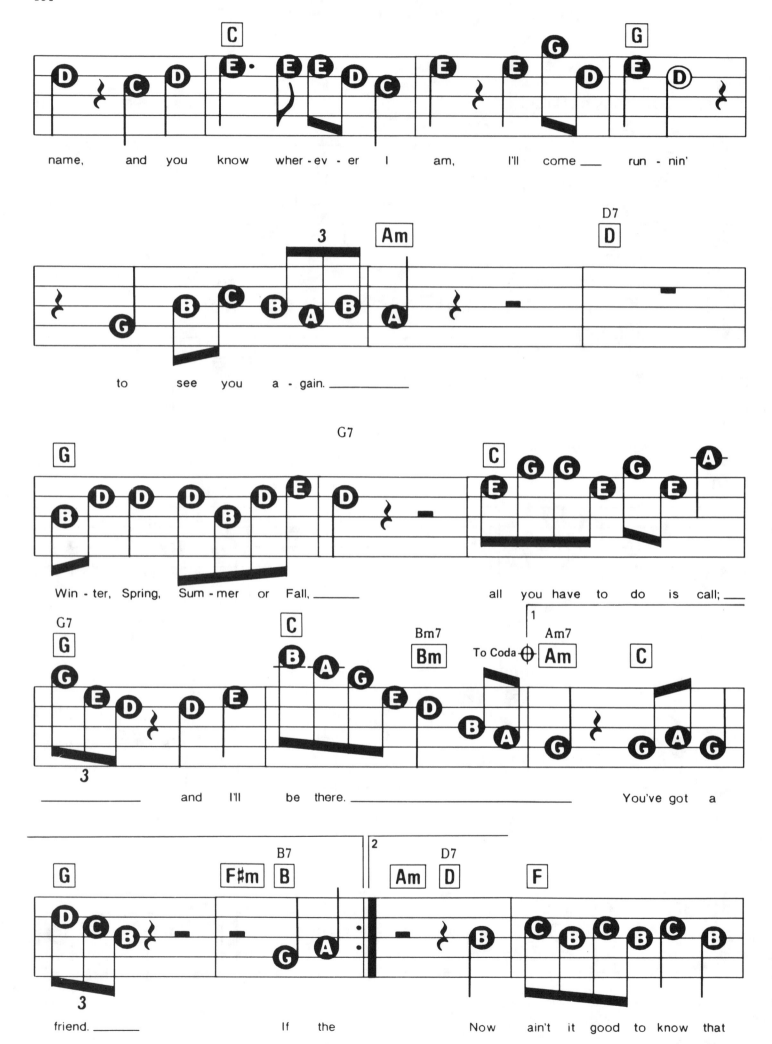

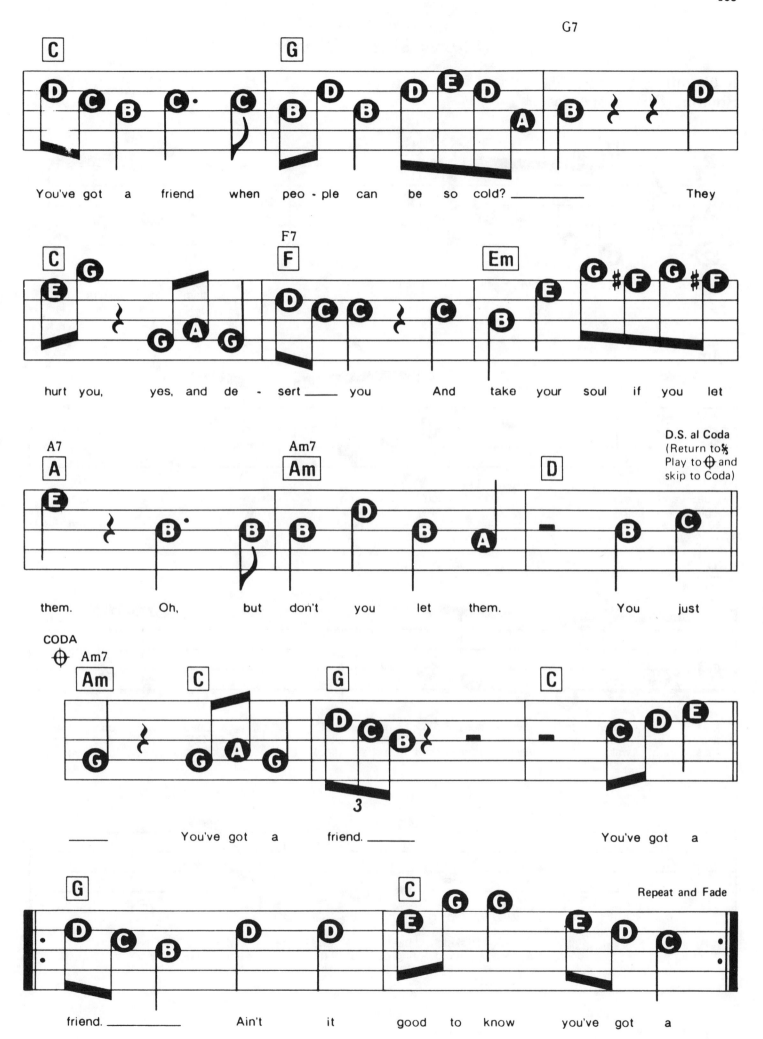

# Vincent
## (Starry Starry Night)

Registration 7
Rhythm: 8 Beat or Pops

Words and Music by
Don McLean

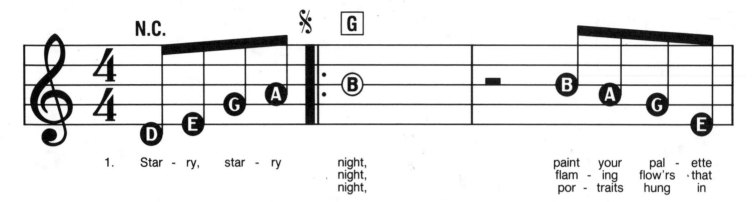

1. Star - ry, star - ry night,
night,
night,

paint your pal - ette
flam - ing flow'rs that
por - traits hung in

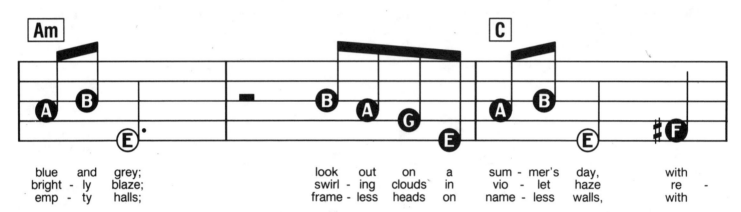

blue and grey;
bright - ly blaze;
emp - ty halls;

look out on a sum - mer's day, with
swirl - ing clouds in vio - let haze re -
frame - less heads on name - less walls, with

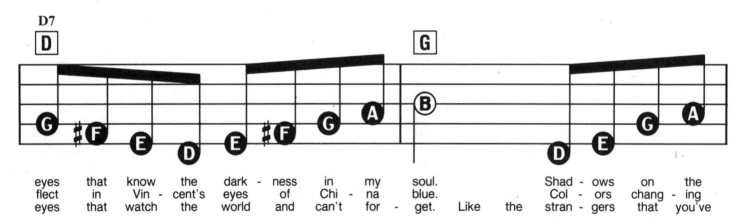

eyes that know the dark - ness in my soul.
flect in Vin - cent's eyes of Chi - na blue.
eyes that watch the world and can't for - get.

Shad - ows on the
Col - ors chang - ing
Like the stran - gers that you've

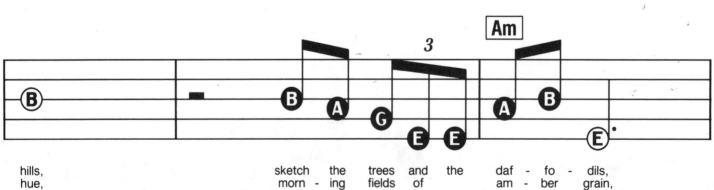

hills,
hue,
met,

sketch the trees and the daf - fo - dils,
morn - ing fields of am - ber grain,
the rag - ged men in rag - ged clothes,

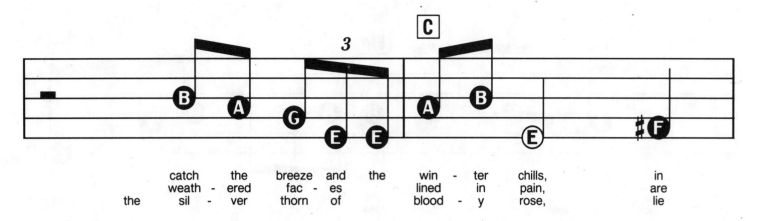

catch the breeze and the win - ter chills, in
weath - ered fac - es lined in pain, are
the sil - ver thorn of blood - y rose, lie

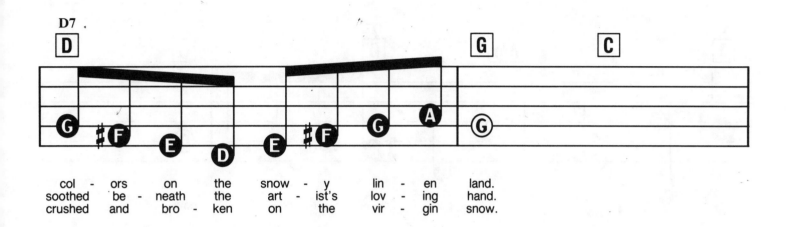

col - ors on the snow - y lin - en land.
soothed be - neath the art - ist's lov - ing hand.
crushed and bro - ken on the vir - gin snow.

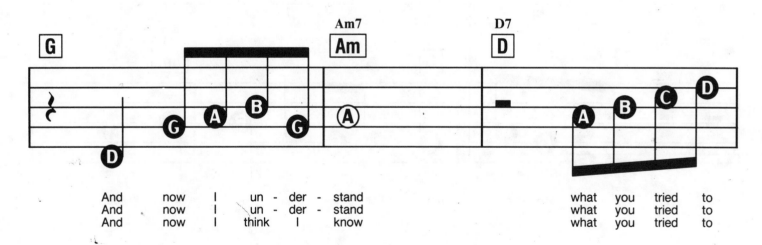

And now I un - der - stand what you tried to
And now I un - der - stand what you tried to
And now I think I know what you tried to

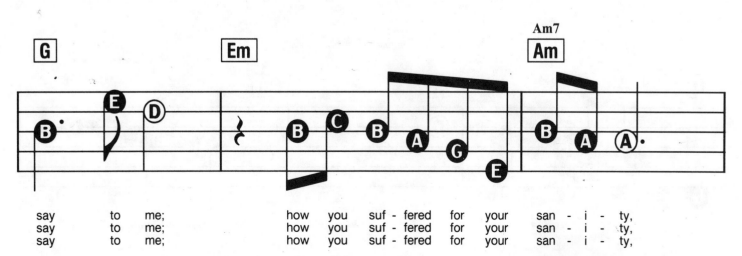

say to me; how you suf - fered for your san - i - ty,
say to me; how you suf - fered for your san - i - ty,
say to me; how you suf - fered for your san - i - ty,

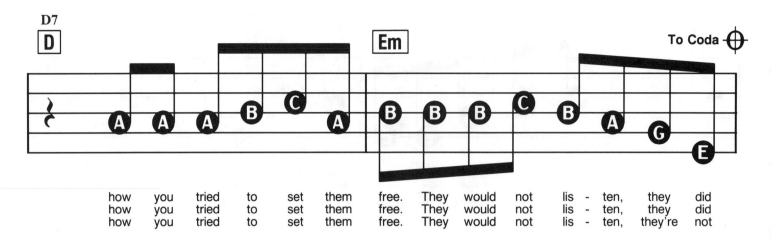

how you tried to set them free. They would not lis - ten, they did
how you tried to set them free. They would not lis - ten, they did
how you tried to set them free. They would not lis - ten, they're not

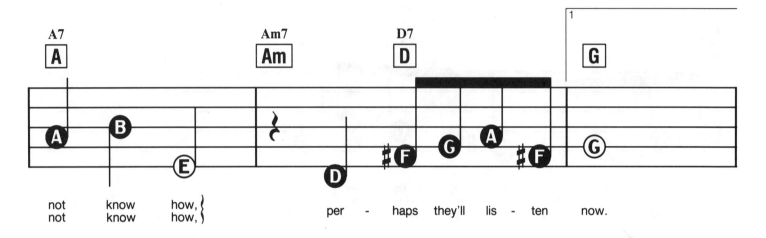

not know how, per - haps they'll lis - ten now.
not know how,

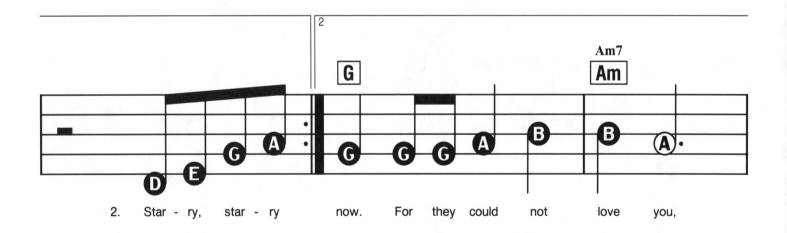

2. Star - ry, star - ry now. For they could not love you,

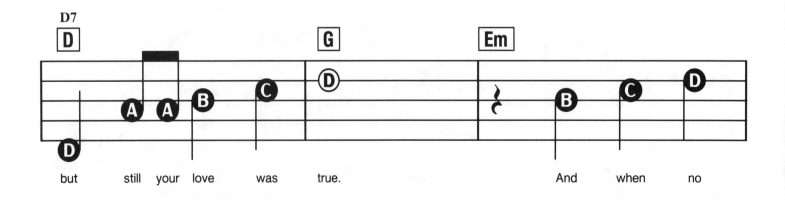

but still your love was true. And when no

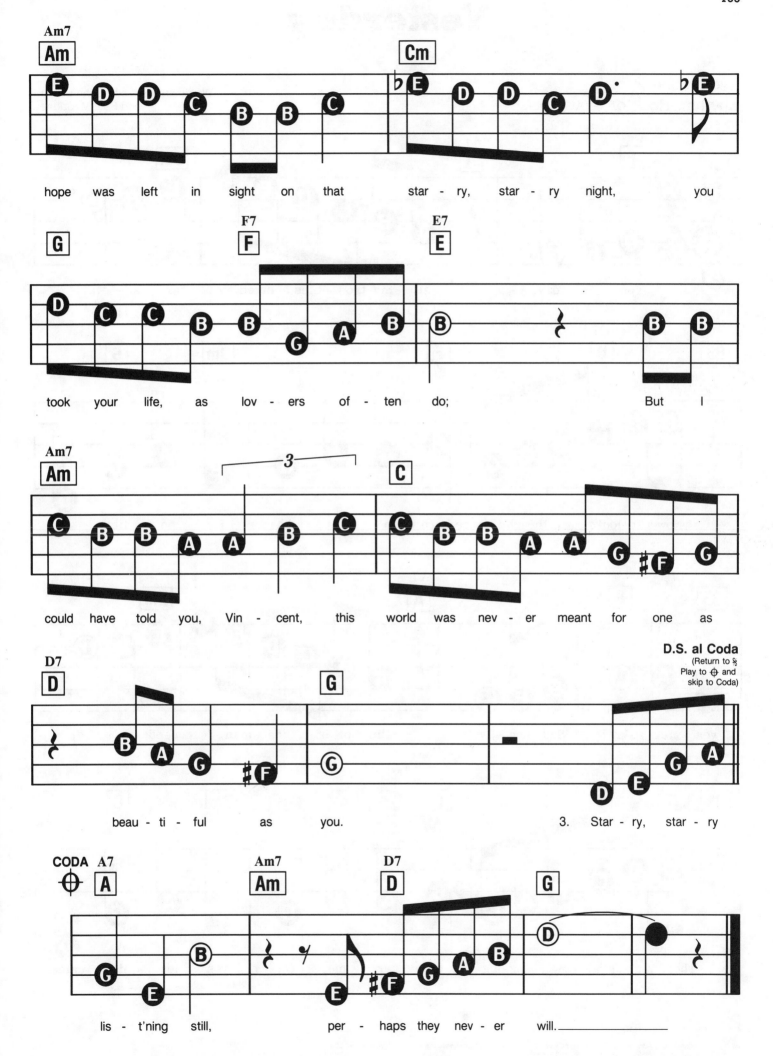

# Yesterday

Registration 2
Rhythm: Rock or Slow Rock

Words and Music by John Lennon
and Paul McCartney

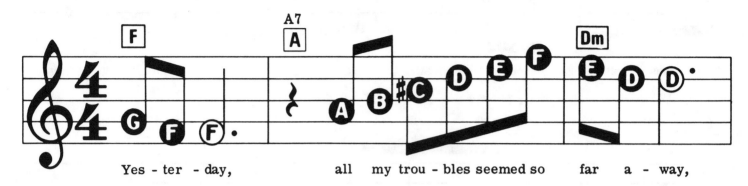

Yes - ter - day, all my trou - bles seemed so far a - way,

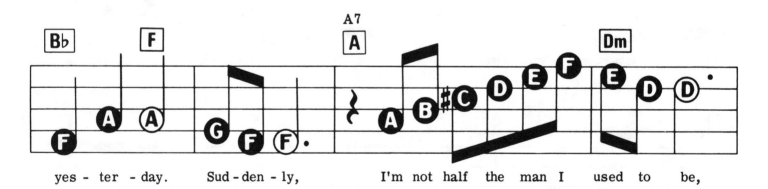

Now it looks as though they're here to stay, Oh I be - lieve in

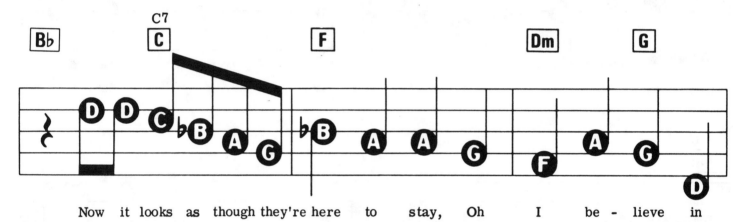

yes - ter - day. Sud - den - ly, I'm not half the man I used to be,

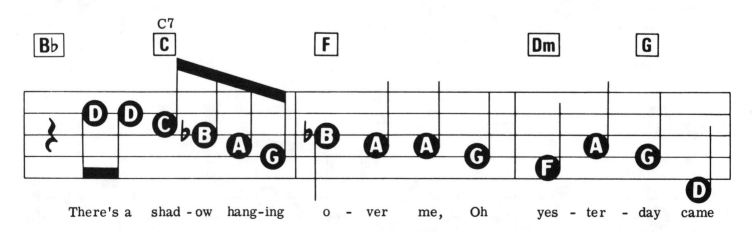

There's a shad - ow hang - ing o - ver me, Oh yes - ter - day came

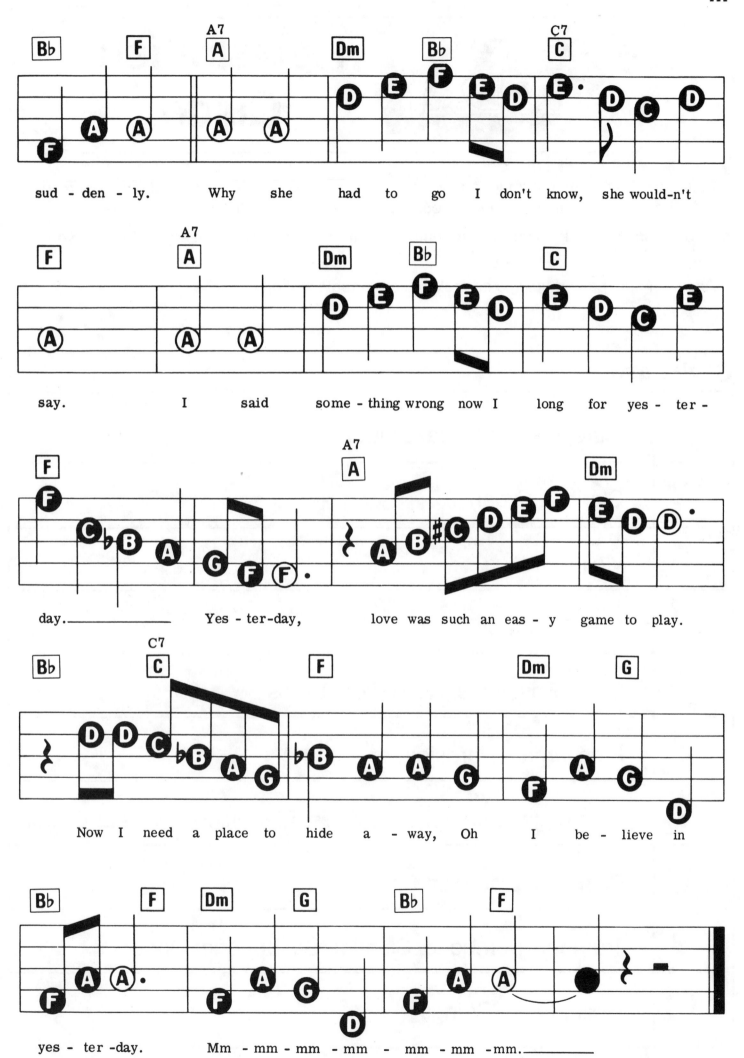

# Registration Guide

- Match the Registration number on the song to the corresponding numbered category below. Select and activate an instrumental sound available on your instrument.

- Choose an automatic rhythm appropriate to the mood and style of the song. (Consult your Owner's Guide for proper operation of automatic rhythm features.)

- Adjust the tempo and volume controls to comfortable settings.

## Registration

| | |
|---|---|
| **1** | Flute, Pan Flute, Jazz Flute |
| **2** | Clarinet, Organ |
| **3** | Violin, Strings |
| **4** | Brass, Trumpet |
| **5** | Synth Ensemble, Accordion, Brass |
| **6** | Pipe Organ, Harpsichord |
| **7** | Jazz Organ, Vibraphone, Vibes, Electric Piano, Jazz Guitar |
| **8** | Piano, Electric Piano |
| **9** | Trumpet, Trombone, Clarinet, Saxophone, Oboe |
| **10** | Violin, Cello, Strings |